Remote Usability Testing

Actionable insights in user behavior across geographies and time zones

Inge De Bleecker
Rebecca Okoroji

BIRMINGHAM - MUMBAI

Remote Usability Testing

Commissioning Editor: Amarabha Banerjee
Acquisition Editor: Siddharth Mandal
Content Development Editor: Mohammed Yusuf Imaratwale
Technical Editor: Shweta Jadhav
Copy Editor: Safis Editing
Project Coordinator: Hardik Bhinde
Proofreader: Safis Editing
Indexer: Pratik Shirodkar
Graphics: Jason Monteiro, Nic Gruchot
Production Coordinator: Shraddha Falebhai

First published: August 2018

Production reference: 1170818

Published by Packt Publishing Ltd.
Livery Place
35 Livery Street
Birmingham
B3 2PB, UK.

ISBN 978-1-78899-904-5

www.packtpub.com

To all our colleagues and clients over the years; this book would not exist without you.

– Inge De Bleecker and Rebecca Okoroji

`mapt.io`

Mapt is an online digital library that gives you full access to over 5,000 books and videos, as well as industry leading tools to help you plan your personal development and advance your career. For more information, please visit our website.

Why subscribe?

- Spend less time learning and more time coding with practical eBooks and Videos from over 4,000 industry professionals

- Improve your learning with Skill Plans built especially for you

- Get a free eBook or video every month

- Mapt is fully searchable

- Copy and paste, print, and bookmark content

PacktPub.com

Did you know that Packt offers eBook versions of every book published, with PDF and ePub files available? You can upgrade to the eBook version at `www.PacktPub.com` and as a print book customer, you are entitled to a discount on the eBook copy. Get in touch with us at `service@packtpub.com` for more details.

At `www.PacktPub.com`, you can also read a collection of free technical articles, sign up for a range of free newsletters, and receive exclusive discounts and offers on Packt books and eBooks.

Contributors

About the authors

Inge De Bleecker has been designing and testing web, mobile, and voice experiences for more than 20 years. She builds and leads UX teams and evangelizes UX throughout organizations. She is fascinated by the communication between humans and devices. Her mantras are "design for everyone" and "test early and often." Inge has run over 200 remote studies across different industries, languages, and regions. She finds remote studies a powerful and effective way to gather user feedback that would otherwise be difficult to collect.

Rebecca and I would both like to thank Packt Publishing for their encouragement and support throughout this exciting experience. Rebecca, it was a true joy collaborating with you, as always! Thanks also to my husband, Arpit, my son, Kennas, and my parents for their unfailing love, support, and patience.

Rebecca Okoroji has been working in UX since 2000. She is passionate about the need for providing exceptional digital experiences and has since expanded her focus to encompass customer experience. She believes that there is no such thing as a user error, only badly designed interfaces. Customer/user feedback is essential to building a good UX, and remote unmoderated usability testing is a cost-effective and efficient way of collecting this. Rebecca has conducted over 100 such studies in globally dispersed projects for a large variety of industries and has a wealth of experience to draw on.

Inge and I would both like to thank our reviewers for their great feedback, and very especially Nic for the beautiful images she designed. Writing this book with Inge was more fun than I could ever have imagined. Thank you for that, Inge! Additionally, I would like to thank my husband for never doubting that this would be an exhilarating, at times tear-my-hair-out frustrating, but ultimately gratifying adventure.

About the reviewers

UX blogger, author of *Fixing Bad UX Design* (Packt Publishing), author of the chapter about *UX for Conversion* for a Brazilian book on digital marketing, reviewer of the book *UX Mobile* (Packt Publishing), **Lisandra Maioli** is an Italian-Brazilian journalist with a certification in UX (General Assembly LA), a post-graduate diploma in Marketing (UC Berkeley), in digital marketing (UCLA), in Interactive Digital Medias (Senac SP), and in Digital-Cultural Journalism (PUC SP). She has about two decades of international and multidisciplinary experience in digital communications in different roles, working for different companies and clients based in Brazil, the US, Italy, Ireland, China, Germany, and the Netherlands.

Jens Jacobsen created his first web page in 1995 with Notepad and tested it in NCSA Mosaic. Soon, he shifted his focus from coding to conceptual work and wrote a book on the conceptual design of websites, Website-Konzeption, published in German by Addison-Wesley in 2001. It is now in its 8th edition. Jens writes for several German expert blogs about usability, UX, and creating successful websites. He works as a freelance UX consultant for mid- and big-sized companies.

Packt is searching for authors like you

If you're interested in becoming an author for Packt, please visit `authors.packtpub.com` and apply today. We have worked with thousands of developers and tech professionals, just like you, to help them share their insight with the global tech community. You can make a general application, apply for a specific hot topic that we are recruiting an author for, or submit your own idea.

Table of Contents

Preface 1

Chapter 1: Why Everyone Should Run Remote Usability Studies 5
  Usability testing methodologies 6
    In-person or lab usability testing 7
    Remote usability testing 7
      Advantages of remote methods 8
        Extended reach 9
        Typical devices 9
        No travel required 9
        No travel costs 9
        No lab costs 10
        No lab environment 10
        Familiar equipment 10
        User's natural environment 10
        In the wild testing 11
        Larger number of participants 11
      Disadvantages of remote methods 11
        Distributing the product under testing 11
        Other disadvantages 12
    Remote moderated usability testing 12
      Advantages of remote moderated studies 12
        Body language 13
        Tailored follow-up questions 13
      Disadvantages of remote moderated studies 13
    Remote unmoderated usability testing 13
      Advantages of remote unmoderated studies 13
        Natural behavior 14
        Time zone independent 14
        Less effort for the UX researcher 14
        Eliminates influence 14
        No schedules to manage 15
        Testing with minors 15
        Faster turnaround 15
      Disadvantages of remote unmoderated studies 15
        Guidance 15
        Other disadvantages 16
  Types of usability studies 16
    Formative and summative usability studies 17
    Qualitative and quantitative usability studies 17
    Longitudinal and single-session studies 18
    Comparative and single test object studies 18
    Other study types 19
  Summary 19

Chapter 2: What Not to Forget When Planning Your Study   21
  Who are the stakeholders?   22
  The product being tested   22
  The goal of the study   23
    Determining the status quo   24
    A regular study to measure against a baseline   24
    Why? (Finding answers to questions about increasing conversion/decreasing drop-off)   25
    Understanding the users   26
    Global suitability   26
    Comparing design options   26
    Comparing to competitors   27
    Feature validation   27
    Concept validation   28
    Product validation   28
    What to do next   28
    Predicting future behavior   29
    Classic usability goals   29
  The budget   30
  The scope of the study (the tasks and questions)   30
    Objective benchmark scores   32
      Task completion rate   32
      Time-on-task   32
    Subjective benchmark scores   32
      Customer Effort Score   32
      Single Ease Question   32
      Task satisfaction rate   32
      Net Promoter Score   33
      System Usability Scale   33
      USERindex   33
  The test environment   34
    Which are the target devices for the study?   34
    What state is the product in?   35
    How can the product be accessed?   35
    Are special credentials required?   36
    Are there any known bugs?   36
    Any other requirements   36
  The participants   37
    Demographic requirements   37
    Device requirements   38
    Other criteria   38
    The number of participants   39
    Participant incentives/compensation   41
  The study methodology   41
    Moderated or unmoderated study   41
    Video-based and survey-based studies   41

The schedule 42
    When will the product be available for testing? 42
    Are there any hard deadlines? 42
    Are there any update cycles that need to be taken into consideration? 43
    Do the participants need to be equipped with physical devices? 43
    What time of year is the study planned for? 43
    Is a pilot run with participants/stakeholders necessary? 44
    Is external approval required? 44
    Do external factors impose a schedule on the UX study? 44
The deliverables 45
    Study framework for sign off 45
    Participant screener 45
    Discussion guide/script 45
    Report 45
Next steps 46
Summary 46
Chapter 3: How to Effectively Recruit Participants 49
Who to recruit 49
    Multiple target user groups 50
    When the target user (almost) doesn't exist 51
    Recruiting for specific target user groups 51
        Minors 51
        Seniors 52
        People with disabilities 52
        Subject matter experts 52
    Who is really participating in your study? 53
How to find participants 53
    Self-recruiting 54
        Coworkers 54
        Friends and family 54
        Recruiting Ads 55
        Customers 55
    Panel companies 55
        Representations of target users 56
        Expectations 56
Screening the participants 56
    Screener methods 57
    The number of participants 57
    Challenges 57
Informing the participants 58
    Time commitments 59
    Location 59
    Online versus offline 59
    Devices and tools 60
    Expectations 60

Compensation   61
  Monetary compensation   61
    Cash   61
    Gift cards   61
    Donations   62
  Non-monetary compensation   62
    Lottery drawings   62
    Promotional items   62
    Sheer gratitude   62
  How much is the right amount?   63
  When to provide compensation   63
  Extra costs   64

Next steps   64
  Re-screening participants   64
  Building a database for future recruiting   65
Summary   66

Chapter 4: Running a Remote Moderated Study   67
Discussion guide   68
  Anatomy of a discussion guide   68
    Introduction   69
    Warm-up   69
    Tasks   70
      How many tasks and questions?   70
      Task descriptions   70
      Topics   71
      Questions   72
    Post-session questions   74
    Wrap-up   74
  Writing tips   74
    Tone   75
    Style   75
Preparing for the study   75
  Number of participants   76
  Days for the sessions   76
  Product being tested   76
  Internal team   76
  Number of sessions per day   76
    Time of day   77
    Dry run   77
      Backup slots   77
      Floaters   78
      Sample schedule   78
  Communicating   78
    Communicating with observers   79
    Communicating with participants   79
    Communication tools   79
    Being prepared for changes   79
  Pre-session tech setup   80
Running the study   80

Running the sessions   81
When to abort a session   81
   The participant is not getting it   81
   Mismatches in participants   81
      Someone other than the recruited participant joins the session   82
      Participant misrepresented themselves   82
Debriefing   82
When enough is enough   82
   Blocking usability issues   83
   Consistent feedback   83
Moderator techniques   83
   The rules of the game   83
   Understanding your participants   84
      Level of engagement   84
      Participant disposition   85
   Managing observers   86
   Moderator note-taking   86
Basic tool functionality   87
Next steps   87
Summary   88
Chapter 5: Running a Remote Unmoderated Study with User Videos   89
About user videos   90
Screen capture   90
Audio capture   90
   Think-aloud protocol   91
      Formulating thoughts   91
      Continued thinking aloud   91
Strengths of user videos   92
   Observation of user actions   92
   Think-aloud verbal cues   92
   Facial expressions   92
   A picture is worth a thousand words   92
   Suitable throughout the development cycle   92
Limitations of user videos   92
   Privacy of user data   93
   Digital rights management (DRM)   93
   Less deliberate feedback   93
Session organization   94
   Session duration   94
   Number of participants   95
   Number of tasks   95
   Number of videos   95
The script   95
Introduction   96
Instructions   96
   Think-aloud   96
      Give examples   97
      Greeting and task description   97

Video recording	98
Video file format, size, and delivery	98
Access to the product under testing	99
Device to be used	99
Read task instructions	99
Tasks	99
Tasks that are easy to complete	99
Tasks that are difficult to complete	100
Complex tasks	100
Long tasks	100
Goal-oriented tasks	101
Post-task or post-session questions	101
Writing tips	102
Provide a clear starting point for each task	102
Tone	102
Preparing for the study	103
Scheduling participants	103
Running the study	104
Next steps	104
Summary	105
Chapter 6: Running a Remote Unmoderated Study with a Survey	107
About surveys	108
Write-down-what-you-think protocol	108
Strengths of surveys	109
Long tasks	109
Deep dive questions	109
Suitable throughout the development cycle	110
Larger number of participants	110
Limitations of surveys	110
Not ideal for path analysis	111
Fraud	111
Self-reported data	112
Survey questions	112
Open questions	113
Closed questions	114
Single-answer multiple-choice questions	115
Multi-answer, multiple-choice questions	118
Semantic differential scale	118
Ranking questions	119
Grouping questions	119
Study organization	120
Session duration	120
Number of participants	121
Number of tasks	121
The script	121
Introduction	121
Instructions	122
Write-down-what-you-think protocol	122

Access to the product under testing | 122
Device to be used | 123
Tasks versus questions | 123
Tasks | 123
Task context | 123
Task flow | 123
Tasks that are easy to complete | 124
Tasks that are difficult to complete | 124
Complex tasks | 125
Long tasks | 125
Goal-oriented tasks | 125
Post-task questions | 125
Time-on-task measurement | 126
Post-session questions | 126
What makes for a good question? | 127
What is the desired answer? | 127
One question per question | 128
Avoiding leading questions | 128
Meeting the goals | 129
Clarity | 129
Tone | 129
Unblocking participants | 129
Providing clear anchors | 129
Providing a clear starting point for each task | 130
Facilitating sentiment expression | 130
Follow-up questions | 130
Obvious questions | 131
Preparing for the study | 131
Dry run | 131
Scheduling participants | 131
Running the study | 132
Next steps | 132
Summary | 133
Chapter 7: Running a Remote Unmoderated Study with a Hybrid Approach | 135
About the hybrid method | 136
Strengths of the hybrid method | 136
Self-reported data informed by user videos | 137
Device and product version confirmation | 137
Reducing fraud | 137
Limitations of the hybrid method | 137
Increased analysis effort for the UX researcher | 138
Study organization | 138
Session duration | 138
Number of participants | 138
Number of tasks | 138
The script | 139

Introduction   139
Instructions   139
   Standalone responses   140
Tasks   140
   Recording start and end   140
   Balance between open questions and user videos   140
   User videos for relevant tasks only   140
Post-task or post-session questions   141
Writing tips   141
Preparing for the study   141
   Scheduling participants   141
Running the study   142
Next steps   142
Summary   142
Chapter 8: What to Consider When Analyzing and Presenting the Study Results   143
  Analyzing the data   143
  Preparing the raw data   143
    Remote moderated studies   143
    Remote unmoderated studies with videos   144
    Remote unmoderated studies with surveys   144
    Hybrid remote unmoderated studies   144
  Compiling the findings   144
    Observed or recorded data   145
    Self-reported data   145
  Interpreting the findings   146
    Visualising the data   146
     (Stacked) column/bar chart   146
     Line chart   148
     Pie chart   149
     Table   151
     Word cloud   151
     Lists   152
     Best practices when representing data   154
    Identifying issues   155
     Where did the study participants struggle with a task?   155
     Where did the participants voice (or respond with) insecurity?   156
     Were there any big emotions, whether negative or positive?   156
     Are there any outliers?   156
     Are participants consistently using different terminology?   156
     Are there any inconsistencies in the responses?   156
     Were there any "false positives"?   157
     Did anyone encounter bugs?   157
  Identifying recommendations   157
    Make recommendations constructive and direct   158
    Provide detail and illustrate   158
    Address only the original usability problem   159
    Speak the readers' language   159
    Provide alternatives   159

Solve the problem 159
Assign a severity 159
Focus on the user 160

Reporting the data 160
Audience 161
Content of the report 161
Cover page 161
Summary 162
The goal(s) 162
Any critical issues 162
The bottom line 162
Optional details 162
Study context 162
Benchmark scores 163
Findings 163
Improvement/remediation recommendations 164
Verbatim participant comments 164
Conclusion and next steps 165
Appendix 165
Summary 165

Chapter 9: Thanks! And What Now? 167
The debrief session 167
Next steps 170
Summary 171

Appendix A: Sample Material and Further Reading 173
Sample material 173
Further reading 173

Other Books You May Enjoy 175

Index 179

Preface

Does the world really need yet another book about usability testing? We believe it does as there are no books available that are focused solely on the very exciting realm of remote usability testing. Hopefully, by the end of this book, we will have convinced you too.

Please take the time to read this preface because we want to ensure that you do not go into the book with expectations that we cannot fulfill. We promise to keep it short.

This book is about remote usability testing, nothing else. It is targeted at anyone interested in understanding why remote usability testing is becoming more ubiquitous in the UX portfolio and how best to plan, run, and wrap up this type of study.

Some housekeeping before we dive in:

- In this book, we use the terms *usability test, usability study*, and *UX study* in the broader sense of user testing, which comprises evaluating product acceptance, the perceived value of features and functionality, usefulness, and much more, and is thus not restricted to the pure evaluation of ease-of-use.
- We use the terms *product*, *interface*, and *digital interface* interchangeably throughout the book when referring to the product under testing.
- Throughout the book, we refer to the person executing the study as the *UX researcher*. The person triggering the study will be referred to as the *study sponsor*. We understand that the actual setup of a usability test with regard to the involved stakeholders may differ from reader to reader. The person running the study may be part of the UX team designing the product under testing or an external consultant contracted only to run the test; the study sponsor and the UX researcher may be one and the same person, and so on. We will stick to these terms and you can translate them into your specific context.
- The book is tool agnostic. There are many tools available that support remote usability testing, but we do not want to recommend any specific software considering how quickly new, updated products are made available. We also believe that UX researchers should use the tools they are most comfortable and familiar with in order to be able to focus completely on the study instead of the tool itself.

That's all! We've had a great time writing this book, and we hope you find it useful.

Inge and Rebecca

Who this book is for

This book targets both User Experience (UX) professionals who are familiar with traditional in-person usability testing methodologies, and UX designers who have had no prior exposure to user research and usability testing. This book may also be of use to customer experience professionals, product managers, or frontend developers who are interested in understanding remote usability testing.

What this book covers

Chapter 1, *Why Everyone Should Run Remote Usability Studies*, explains why there are only very few situations in which a remote usability study would be ill-advised.

Chapter 2, *What Not to Forget When Planning Your Study*, describes how to plan a study, comprising all aspects that will influence its successful execution.

Chapter 3, *How to Effectively Recruit the Right Participants*, outlines how to determine whom to recruit, how to recruit and ensure that they are properly informed.

Chapter 4, *Running a Remote Moderated Study*, describes how to successfully run a remote moderated study.

Chapter 5, *Running a Remote Unmoderated Study with User Videos*, describes how to successfully run a remote unmoderated study using user videos.

Chapter 6, *Running a Remote Unmoderated Study with a Survey*, describes how to successfully run a remote unmoderated study using surveys.

Chapter 7, *Running a Remote Unmoderated Study with a Hybrid Approach*, describes how to successfully run a remote unmoderated study using a hybrid approach of user videos and surveys. This chapter builds on the previous two chapters.

Chapter 8, *What to Consider When Analyzing and Presenting the Study Results*, gives guidelines on writing reports that will help the audience understand the study results and empathize with the users' experience.

Chapter 9, *Thanks! And What Now?*, talks about possible next steps once the study results have been evaluated and, optionally, documented.

To get the most out of this book

The reader does not need to have any prior experience with usability testing but should be familiar with the concepts of user-centered design.

No software is needed for this book.

Download the color images

We provide a PDF file that has color images of the screenshots/diagrams used in this book. You can download it here: http://www.packtpub.com/sites/default/files/downloads/RemoteUsabilityTesting_ColorImages.pdf.

Conventions used

There are a number of text conventions used throughout this book.

Bold: Indicates a new term, an important word, or words that you see onscreen. For example, words in menus or dialog boxes appear in the text like this. Here is an example: "Select **System info** from the **Administration** panel."

Get in touch

Feedback from our readers is always welcome.

General feedback: Email feedback@packtpub.com and mention the book title in the subject of your message. If you have questions about any aspect of this book, please email us at questions@packtpub.com.

Errata: Although we have taken every care to ensure the accuracy of our content, mistakes do happen. If you have found a mistake in this book, we would be grateful if you would report this to us. Please visit www.packtpub.com/submit-errata, selecting your book, clicking on the Errata Submission Form link, and entering the details.

Piracy: If you come across any illegal copies of our works in any form on the Internet, we would be grateful if you would provide us with the location address or website name. Please contact us at copyright@packtpub.com with a link to the material.

If you are interested in becoming an author: If there is a topic that you have expertise in and you are interested in either writing or contributing to a book, please visit authors.packtpub.com.

Reviews

Please leave a review. Once you have read and used this book, why not leave a review on the site that you purchased it from? Potential readers can then see and use your unbiased opinion to make purchase decisions, we at Packt can understand what you think about our products, and our authors can see your feedback on their book. Thank you!

For more information about Packt, please visit packtpub.com.

Why Everyone Should Run Remote Usability Studies

1

If you are reading this book, then you probably already know what usability testing is, but we don't want to make any assumptions about that, which takes us right to the essence of this book: usability testing is about not making assumptions. In fact, it takes the opposite approach. Usability studies are executed in order to gain concrete, actionable insights. Instead of assuming that users will use an interface in a certain manner, usability tests are run to actually monitor their use of the interface, identify where they stumble and what they appreciate, hear their thoughts, understand their decisions and ultimately use this information to improve the product.

Let's take a step back and talk about usability. Usability refers to how easy an interface is to use. It is a quality that every interface inherently possesses. Issues arise when this quality is not very pronounced. ISO 9241-11 defines usability as the "extent to which a product can be used by specified users to achieve specified goals with effectiveness, efficiency, and satisfaction in a specified context of use".

Effectiveness (how well the user achieves their goal) and efficiency (how much effort is required from the user to achieve their goal) are unsurprising in the ISO description. Satisfaction, however, is interesting: even if an interface is effective (meaning that it does what it needs to do) and efficient (meaning that it does not require a lot of effort to do it), how the user feels about using the interface is also relevant. For every app someone uses, there is probably a plethora of competing apps that do exactly the same thing. So how does the user choose? Oftentimes, they go by the very subjective feeling of being satisfied or not. The evaluation of the usability of an interface is therefore based on both very objective measures, such as the task completion rate or the time spent on a task, but also on the very subjective perception of the individual user using the interface. Did the user like the design? Are the colors pleasing? Does the interface make the user feel good about themselves? Understanding what users like or dislike, where they struggle, and which tasks come easy to them, helps with the following:

- Evaluate the usability of the interface
- Identify areas to fix and patterns to avoid
- Determine a usability baseline across product iterations
- Compare an interface with the competition

A more formal approach to evaluate the usability of a product is to run a usability test. Usability testing refers to "evaluating a product or service by testing it with representative users" (`https://www.usability.gov/how-to-and-tools/methods/usability-testing.html`). Usability testing is a subdiscipline of **User Experience** (**UX**). Its goal is to ensure that a given product is easy to use and that the user's experience with the product is intuitive, useful, and satisfying. Essentially, users, who are representative of the target users, are monitored while using an interface to complete tasks that are relevant to their needs. A usability test can be run at any stage of the product development lifecycle. Usability tests in the early design stages can be used to validate a navigation concept using wireframes, for example, or test the usability of new features using early prototypes, or benchmark the ease-of-use of the final product. The feedback is then used to refine and improve the user interface, ideally in an iterative process.

We want to point out that usability testing is not market research. While usability testing is mostly focused on the interaction with a particular product, market research is usually less specific; usability testing is about ease-of-use, whereas market research is mostly about user opinions or past experience. Usability testing does not require a large number of participants in order to generate valuable results, whereas most market research tools depend on large, statistically relevant sample sets.

Usability testing is also not **Quality Assurance** (**QA**). Quality assurance is performed by qualified testers, whereas usability testing is preferably run with non-QA testers. Quality assurance is aimed at finding bugs, whereas usability testing is preferably run on bug-free implementations. Usability testing usually involves a user completing a task the way they normally would, while quality assurance testers will repeat that same task multiple times in order to mimic every possible permutation a real user might encounter.

Usability testing methodologies

Usability tests can be run in different ways and for various types of studies. Let's first look into the different ways (or methodologies) of executing a usability test. These are mainly differentiated by the following characteristics:

- In-person versus remote
- Moderated versus unmoderated

In-person or lab usability testing

This is the traditional way to run a usability test: users who meet the user profile requirements are invited to participate in a usability study at a lab. This methodology is almost always moderated, meaning that there is always a UX researcher present who moderates the user sessions.

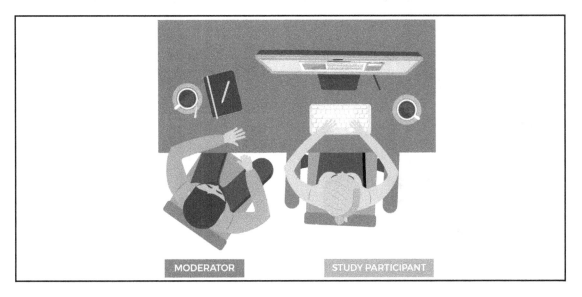

In-person usability testing

We are listing this methodology for completeness, but this book only covers remote methodologies.

Remote usability testing

While in-person usability testing has been around for some time, remote usability testing has only more recently become feasible due to advances in technology and the availability of new tools.

Connectivity and the internet have made it possible for us to run usability studies remotely using software that allows the moderator to view and capture the participant's screen, hear their audio input, and view their faces. Enhanced distribution and recording tools have also made it possible to target participants offline and receive high-fidelity user videos and feedback.

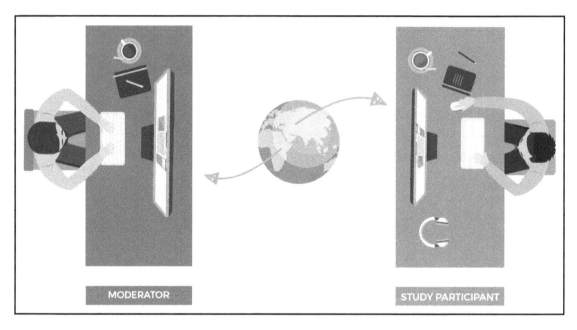

Remote usability testing

Remote usability testing allows companies to gain insights into user behavior in their natural environment and on their own schedule. It involves fewer logistics, allows participation regardless of location, and is quicker and cheaper to execute compared to in-person studies, while still delivering valuable insights and feedback. In today's globally connected world, quickly getting local insights is imperative for providing the same standard of user experience while remaining culturally specific.

Advantages of remote methods

We are raving fans of remote usability testing (you might have guessed this by the fact that we wrote a book about it) for the following reasons.

Extended reach

Remote studies make it easy to include participants from different geographic locations in the same study. Essentially, anyone with a smart device and an internet connection can participate. Imagine that the product under testing is a social app aimed at allowing people to connect with each other when in proximity of another person using the same app. The typical users are city dwellers in densely populated capitals around the globe. Setting up in-person studies in each of the major cities would be logistically complex and expensive. This is where remote studies provide the biggest benefit.

Typical devices

In a remote study, study participants use their own devices. That variety of devices combined with operating system versions (and, optionally, browser versions) and connectivity speeds is near impossible to match in a lab setting. Imagine a wayfinding app that provides directions to a selected target which is meant to be rolled out globally. A remote, globally distributed study will allow the study sponsor to gather realistic feedback with regards to how the app deals with the connectivity available locally on typical devices.

No travel required

It is easier to recruit study participants when there is no travel required as it lowers the hurdle for participants to take part in the study. A remote usability study can be completed within as little as half an hour. Imagine a study for a restaurant supply ordering site where the target user group is restaurant chefs. These folks work so many hours that it is very hard to convince them to travel to a lab. Or imagine a company that develops products that are mostly sold in rural areas, such as farming or harvesting equipment. It will be challenging enough to find participants for this study, let alone asking these participants to travel to an in-person study location.

No travel costs

Requiring participants to travel to a lab not only substantially increases the time required for the participants, but also their compensation. As remote studies eliminate the need to travel to a lab location for both the UX researcher and the participants, the costs associated with travel do not apply.

No lab costs

As no lab space is required, it follows that there are no costs for it. In a remote study, the study participants are either in an environment that they select or one mandated by the study (for example, if the study requires that the participants complete the study at their place of work), but they are never required to come into a lab.

No lab environment

A remote study allows the participant to remain in their own environment using their own devices. Any UX study is by definition an artificial event since participants knowingly sign up to provide feedback. We can reduce the level of artificiality around a study in a number of ways. One significant factor is the participant's surroundings and the devices they are using. The participant will feel more comfortable in their own environment than in a lab environment. Imagine that the website being tested is a banking website and the target users are existing customers. If the study requires that real tasks are completed on the website, participants will probably feel more comfortable displaying their banking details on their screens while in their homes than in a lab.

Familiar equipment

In a remote study, the study participants are required to use their own devices to complete the tasks. This is another significant advantage of the remote methodology because it removes the hurdle of participants having to familiarize themselves with new hardware and/or software. Imagine the usability test of some gaming software. Gamers can be very particular about the equipment they use to play. The remote study allows them to play using the devices they are familiar with, and thus eliminates the hurdle of first having to get used to devices provided to them in a lab. Another relevant scenario is users who require assistive technology, such as a screen reader; using their own devices will ensure that they do not first have to configure settings to suit their individual needs.

User's natural environment

Capturing the participant's own environment can also help discover important aspects of how users might interact with the product. Imagine testing a TV-streaming device. The study sponsor will be interested in understanding the individual setup of the participants' environment, such as where they sit when using the device, what the distance to the TV is, or what lighting is available. These settings are difficult to replicate to everyone's individual taste in a lab.

Interruptions can also provide valuable insight into a product's usability with respect to how easy it is to pick back up after an interruption. This is relevant for any interface that is frequently or typically used in an environment or at a time when interruptions might occur, such as a colleague coming over to the user's desk or the doorbell ringing, and so on.

In the wild testing

In a remote study, it is possible to send participants out into "the wild" and ask them to test an interface in a real situation. Imagine an app for browsing a conference program and navigating within a conference center. Testing the app in the participant's home will probably not yield the same insights as compared to when they are actually using it in the conference halls and trying to find the lecture they are interested in via the built-in GPS function. Another example is a scenario where a customer is ordering ahead and picking up their order in a store or restaurant. Study participants are first asked to use an app or a website to order something and are then asked to go and pick it up. These types of studies provide insight into the broader customer experience, such as how easy it was to match up the order with the orderer, whether the order was ready at the time promised, and so on.

Larger number of participants

As a consequence of the lower costs and effort associated with running a remote study, it is possible to recruit more participants. With a larger number of participants, it is easier to determine the magnitude of any issue that is found.

Disadvantages of remote methods

We see only one main drawback to remote usability studies (although we might be biased as we are raving fans, after all).

Distributing the product under testing

When the product to be tested is not a production version, such as an app that can be downloaded from an app store, a website that is publicly accessible, or a product that the user already owns, the user will have to be adequately equipped. The study sponsor will either have to provide early versions of their designs, their software, or their product to each participant for testing.

This can usually be managed when planning the study, and we will talk about this in more detail in the following chapter. It only proves to be insurmountable when the study sponsor cannot or does not want to share these early versions outside of their lab or company for security or logistical reasons. In this case, only in-person testing is possible.

Other disadvantages

Some people will say that not being able to run the study in a controlled environment, such as a lab, is a disadvantage of remote methodologies, but we would argue that it provides a more natural context to the study. How likely is it that the user of an app will always have a completely quiet environment, with perfect lighting, free of any interruptions when they are using it? No one lives in a vacuum: the phone will ring, someone will be at the door, the participant's child will want attention, and so on. If you remember the definition of usability testing, it states that the interface is tested by "representative users". You can only really judge whether an interface is easy to use when it is being used by the people whom the products target in order to achieve a goal the users would actually have and in the environment that the users would naturally be using the interface in.

Another disadvantage of the remote methodologies that we try to turn into a benefit is that users might run into issues when installing or setting up the interface to be tested. When this setup is identical to how the actual product would be set up, this is valuable feedback regarding how easy it is to get started with the product under testing. However, when the study is based on early prototypes, their installation might require additional time and effort in order to get the participant set up correctly, and this is admittedly more difficult to do remotely than it would be if both parties were present in the same lab together.

Remote moderated usability testing

In a remote moderated usability study, the UX researcher and the study participant are both present and connected, but not physically in the same room. The UX researcher serves as a moderator and observer during the session. Moderated studies use the internet and collaborative software so the UX researcher can moderate and observe the participant's view of the product being tested and their facial expressions if using a webcam.

Advantages of remote moderated studies

All of the advantages of the remote methodologies listed previously apply to the moderated variation as well. In addition, the following are advantages of the remote moderated study when compared to the unmoderated variation.

Body language

If the remote moderated study uses software that allows the UX researcher to see the participant while they are completing the study, the facial expressions and potentially the body language of the participant may provide additional insight and context. This is often considered an advantage of the remote moderated study over the unmoderated variation.

Tailored follow-up questions

The ability to observe the participants in real time as they complete tasks allows the UX researcher, and any study sponsors who are observing remotely, to ask follow-up questions based on what they see. This can provide valuable, additional insights.

Disadvantages of remote moderated studies

The UX researcher has to establish a rapport without personal contact and pastries, although we would argue that the tone of the interaction can also help establish a rapport.

Remote unmoderated usability testing

In a remote unmoderated usability study, the UX researcher sets up the UX study and analyzes the results, but contrary to the moderated version, the study participants participate when it is convenient for them to do so, and without the moderation of the UX researcher. This allows the study participants to complete the study tasks where and when it is most natural to them.

Advantages of remote unmoderated studies

All of the advantages of the remote methodologies listed previously apply to the unmoderated variation as well. In addition, the following are advantages of remote unmoderated studies when compared to the moderated variation.

Natural behavior

Not being in a lab will already allow the participants to feel less inhibited and under observation, but remote unmoderated studies allow the participants to act completely natural. Imagine a music-streaming app. Ideally, the participants should use the app where and when they would naturally use it. This may be while working out or riding a bike, or even doing household chores. Participants might feel inhibited to work out or dance while being observed by a UX researcher. An unmoderated study has both the benefit that the participants can complete the study at their own convenience using the product as naturally as possible while also enabling the UX researcher to gather valuable feedback regarding the use of the app under real conditions. This is the biggest benefit of the remote unmoderated usability study.

Time zone independent

Remote unmoderated studies are independent of time zones. This is especially relevant for globally distributed studies where the study participants are located in varying time zones. In an unmoderated study, there is no interaction required between the UX researcher and the participants, thereby allowing them to complete the study at a time that suits them.

Less effort for the UX researcher

The effort for the UX researcher conducting a remote unmoderated study is significantly less than it would be if they were conducting a remote moderated study. This is because, while the effort for preparing and reporting on the study are comparable, no dedicated sessions between the UX researcher and each participant are required.

Eliminates influence

The absence of a joint session eliminates any inadvertent influence on the study participant by the UX researcher. The validity of the data could be compromised by as subtle an influence as a sigh, or obviously taking notes, for example. Moderating a usability study requires a skilled moderator who is experienced enough to know when to jump in and when to hold back. Remote unmoderated studies can be run by UX researchers who do not necessarily have this experience.

No schedules to manage

In an unmoderated study, no effort is required for scheduling the sessions between the moderator and the participants. In order to handle no-shows, moderated studies very often use "floaters". These floaters are on standby in case someone arrives late or doesn't show up. Managing these schedules and the floaters generates a lot of overhead, not to mention the cost of having additional participants on standby. This effort and cost are absent in remote unmoderated studies.

Testing with minors

Testing with children is easier in remote unmoderated studies because parents can observe their kids and respond to their questions. Imagine a usability study where the product under testing is an educational app targeted at three- to six-year-olds. In an unmoderated study, the parents can be more flexible in interrupting the study and attending to their children if they might have lost patience or interest in the app, and resume the study at a later point in time.

Faster turnaround

The reduced effort required for remote unmoderated studies makes them faster to complete and easier to integrate into iterative testing processes.

Disadvantages of remote unmoderated studies

There is one main disadvantage of remote unmoderated studies when compared with moderated ones.

Guidance

Participants in an unmoderated study require guidance in the form of a script to let them know what they are required to do. This script requires a lot more attention to get it right than a discussion guide for a moderated session. This is obvious when you look at the advantages of this method: The fact that the participants are geographically dispersed and complete the tasks on their own schedule makes it impossible for the UX researcher to be available to guide them through any bit of the study that may be unclear or a dead end that they may inadvertently encounter. In our experience, this is the biggest stumbling point for UX researchers who are comfortable with in-person usability testing and wish to try out the remote unmoderated variety.

The scripts need to cater to any and every outcome, given that there is no possibility to help the participants during the study. You cannot always be sure what the participants are seeing and whether they are exactly where you expect them to be, so you have to anticipate each possible path and cater for it. This is not an insurmountable disadvantage; it just requires more effort and skill on the part of the UX researcher.

Other disadvantages

Another disadvantage of remote unmoderated studies as compared to moderated testing is the lack of immediate observation. Body posture and other physical expressions that could provide the moderator with additional insight during a study are not available. We don't view this as an absolute argument against remote unmoderated testing because you could also argue that, especially in globally distributed tests, the UX researcher may not be familiar with local gestures, and thus potentially interpret them wrongly. In India, for example, shaking your head does not mean "no"—it actually means "ok" or "I understand". Thus, asking participants to explicitly express their opinions in writing in an unmoderated study is less subject to bias than interpreting body language.

The lack of personal contact could also be viewed as a disadvantage because the unmoderated study does not allow for building a strong personal rapport between the UX researcher and the study participants. To some extent, it is possible to build a rapport in a remote unmoderated study just through how the participants are addressed in the script. As we saw with the previously mentioned disadvantage, though, what might help to build rapport with members of one culture might not work with others, or might even have the opposite effect.

One last disadvantage of the remote unmoderated methodology is that it is not possible to get reliable time-on-task values. Some unmoderated testing platforms may record the time taken on a task, but there is no guarantee that this will be valid because it is not possible to determine whether the participant continuously worked on the task or was distracted by a phone call during the execution of the task, for example.

Types of usability studies

In addition to the usability testing methodologies, there are also different types of studies that can be executed using the various methodologies:

- Formative (exploratory) versus summative (assessment)
- Qualitative versus quantitative

- Longitudinal studies versus single session
- Comparative studies versus single product under testing

These types are not mutually exclusive: For example, a comparative study can also be a formative study and a longitudinal study can also be a qualitative study.

Formative and summative usability studies

The difference between formative and summative studies is determined by the development stage of the interface to be tested and the goal of the test. Formative, or exploratory, studies are run on early versions of the product when it is still being designed with the aim of understanding user behavior, needs, and wants, and how people expect to interact with the product while summative, or assessment, studies are run on half-completed to completed products, with the aim of validating the improvements made as a result of previous formative tests, validating individual features or determining a baseline usability. Formative studies are run to shape the product while summative studies are run to assess its usability. Jeff Sauro describes this as follows:

> *"Summative tells you how usable an interface is and formative tells you what isn't usable."*
>
> *– Jeff Sauro* (`https://measuringu.com/formative-summative/`)

Both types are compatible with remote methodologies.

Qualitative and quantitative usability studies

Qualitative and quantitative types of study differ in the type of data that they gather. Qualitative usability studies are focused on gaining in-depth understanding based on narrative data, while quantitative studies collect numerical data in order to produce statistically relevant metrics. A qualitative study will uncover usability issues and identify why users stumble there, whereas quantitative studies will determine the task completion rate, the time-on-task, the users' satisfaction, or other relevant metrics.

A small number of participants is sufficient to provide valuable results in qualitative studies, whereas quantitative studies rely on large numbers of participants in order to provide statistically relevant metrics. How many participants are actually required for a quantitative study is determined by the study parameters, whereas qualitative studies can be run with as few as five participants, according to Nielsen (`https://www.nngroup.com/articles/how-many-test-users/`).

Both study types are compatible with remote methodologies.

Longitudinal and single-session studies

In a single-session study, the participant is only required to participate once in order to complete the study, while a longitudinal study is run over a longer period of time and includes repeated contact with the participants during this time. This time period can be anything from a couple of days to weeks. The study participants are asked to use a product over that period of time. If the aim of the longitudinal study is that the participants record their behavior around and with the interface, this type of study is called a diary study.

Both longitudinal and single-session studies are compatible with remote methodologies.

Comparative and single test object studies

These studies differ in the number of interfaces that are being tested. Single test object studies will cover only a single product, while comparative studies involve two or more products in order to compare them. Comparative studies may be run in order to determine which alternative of a product's early design better reflects the user's expectations. The aim of this type of study is to either find a preferred candidate or identify the best aspects of either alternative which can then be used to drive the further design of the product. Comparative studies can also be used to determine how competing products measure up against each other.

Another aspect of comparative studies is whether all study participants will test all test objects (within-subjects) or whether each study participant only tests one of the test objects (between-subjects). Both have their advantages and disadvantages; fewer participants are required for a within-subject study, but the study duration is necessarily longer, while a between-subjects study eliminates anchoring bias (judging subsequent test objects by comparing them to the subjective baseline made after using the first one).

Comparative studies and studies of a single test object are compatible with remote methodologies.

Other study types

There are other, more specific, study types. One such example is the end-to-end, multichannel customer experience study. A remote unmoderated survey approach works well in gathering data on an end-to-end customer experience that includes a digital and a physical aspect; one example of an activity that includes such aspects could be ordering pizza from a fast food chain on a mobile app and then picking it up at the restaurant. The study can evaluate the ease of installing and registering on the app; ordering food, paying, and selecting the pick-up location; the quality of the messages received apropos pickup time; and the order completion progress, if available. For the actual physical pickup, the study can gather feedback on the punctuality of the order, whether it was clear where to go to pick it up in the restaurant, what information was needed to verify the identity of the orderer, and whether it was fulfilled correctly.

Summary

The advantages of remote usability studies significantly outweigh the disadvantages. A strength of this methodology is the ease of testing across geographical areas. There are only very few situations where a remote usability study would be ill-advised.

In the next chapter, we will look into how to go about planning a remote usability study in order to prepare the foundations for a successful study.

2
What Not to Forget When Planning Your Study

A usability study can be executed without any prior planning, and it is possible that it will still uncover useful insights. Nevertheless, similar to any project approach, following a process and planning the various steps are critical success factors. There is no downside to planning a study upfront. The time and effort involved help to prevent unnecessary discussions down the line, a misalignment of study goals, and unhappiness with deliverables.

Communication is key to successfully completing a remote usability study. All stakeholders have to be in agreement about the framework of the study. That framework consists of the following elements:

- The product being tested
- The goal, budget, and scope of the study
- The test environment
- The participants
- The study methodology
- The schedule
- The deliverables

Each study should be kicked off with a session involving all of the stakeholders in order to establish a consensus on the framework of the study and to set the right expectations for the execution and the expected results. Ideally, the stakeholders will be kept aware of the progress of the study, and will perhaps be involved in its execution.

Who are the stakeholders?

As the word implies, a stakeholder is anyone that has a stake in the interface that is being tested. Stakeholders can include (but are not limited to) the following:

- Upper management (especially for new products)
- The product manager and owner of the interface
- The engineering and development team
- The UX team
- The design team
- The marketing team
- The sales team

In a small company or a company that is new to usability testing, the stakeholders can be virtually anyone within that company: the CEO, a UX contractor, product management, and even the quality assurance team. In larger companies, especially those with more experience in usability testing, the stakeholders are often representatives of the in-house UX and UI teams or the product owner, if the company does not have a dedicated UX team.

Whether or not each of these potential stakeholders needs to be involved will be determined by the UX researcher, and is very specific to each company.

The product being tested

The UX researcher running the usability study has to thoroughly understand the interface that will be tested. This is a prerequisite for being able to write an effective discussion guide or script. The following are some questions that we like to ask the study sponsor during a kick-off session:

- **How would you describe the purpose of the interface?**: Admittedly, it's rare that we don't have any idea what the product does before we start a usability study, but it is always useful (and interesting) to understand how the study sponsor views it. In extreme cases, this view may strongly deviate from the UX researcher's perception of the product. An unnecessary discussion can be avoided by asking the actual users in the study how they perceive the product.
- **What are the most important functions of the product?**: This answers the question of the user's goal. Nobody installs an app because they want to create a user account. It is a necessary means to an end – the end being the actual function that the app provides.

- **How often will the product be used in a normal user scenario?**: A website, such as one for purchasing a ski pass, will, in most likelihood, be used once a year, maybe in repeated succession; a website to read email might be used multiple times daily. This is relevant information for the UX researcher, because how usable a site is influences how quickly a user masters it the first time he visits, and also how quickly he familiarizes himself over repeated usage. Repeated use allows an interface to correct a potentially bad first impression.
- **What are the most frequent use cases?**: The most frequently used functions should be easily recognizable and directly accessible in the product interface. For studies with a wide scope, this information will help to prioritize which tasks are of higher significance.
- **What are known pain points?**: We like asking this question because we usually receive a flood of input. Don't get us wrong here: the UX researcher should not base the study on this very biased input. Instead, they should treat the known pain points as candidates to validate when reviewing the interface themselves.
- **Who are the main competitors?**: This question is especially relevant during a comparative study with competitive sites, but even in other types of studies, it can be relevant input. Similar to the question about the purpose of the interface, this question helps the UX researcher understand how the study sponsor views the product when compared to the competition. Beyond that, it might also be useful to know what similar interfaces the participants are familiar with (and perhaps already using), in order to measure the product under testing against them.

Getting answers to these questions will give the UX researcher a high-level understanding of the product to be tested, its purpose, its core functions, and its subjective position in the market. Before drafting the discussion guide or script, however, we recommend that the UX researcher perform a review of the interface themselves, in order to identify potential weaknesses that the study can validate or refute.

The goal of the study

At the start of a study, its goals must be clear. The goals drive most of the other elements of the framework.

Goals can be anything from all-encompassing (wanting a general feel of how usable a website is) to very specific (wanting to evaluate a new feature and how the users like it, or why the conversion rate went down after a website redesign). At this point in the study, it is more important to ensure that the goals are realistic (that is, that they can actually be achieved with a usability study) than very detailed.

For example, if the goal is to evaluate whether a new marketplace website can go live in its current state, then the goal is not feasible for a usability study: the study can only provide results about the usability of the website, and while we absolutely agree that usability should be a strong deciding factor, a go-live decision for a marketplace website should also be based on whether the product catalog is complete and relevant to customers, for example. The role of the UX researcher is to educate the stakeholders as to what can actually be achieved with a usability study and to get a consensus on that. The study will then be tailored to achieve those goals. It is imperative that everyone involved understands and agrees with the goals.

It is also important to document the goals so that all subsequent steps can refer back to them. It sets the focus for the study, and, while designing the discussion guide/script, the UX researcher should regularly refer back to the goal, in order to validate that the discussion guide/script is on track and hasn't wandered off. When writing up the report, we recommend always referring back to the original goal and documenting whether it has been refuted or validated, based on the results of the study.

The high-level goal of the study has to be unambiguous; details, however, can be flushed out when designing the discussion guide/script. The goal can also be comprised of multiple goals, such as testing a new feature while also testing possible icons that will be used to link to the feature.

The following sections will cover some goals that we have encountered during our usability studies, and how we rate the suitability of each.

Determining the status quo

The following are some verbatim UX study goals that we have heard for determining the usability status quo:

- "Because we have never done it before."
- "We suspect there are usability issues."
- "The flow is horrible, and we believe we are losing users at this step."
- "The intention is to completely redesign the app and website. We need an overview of where we are currently, as a benchmark to measure against later."
- "Ranking of the current functions."

All of these are valid goals, and we heartily support the endeavor to determine a baseline against which future versions can be measured.

A regular study to measure against a baseline

The following are goals that we have encountered when UX studies were initiated to measure the evolution of the product's usability against a baseline:

- "We've implemented all of the recommendations from the previous study to improve the usability, and we now want to determine whether the users appreciate the changes."

- "It's time for our quarterly usability study."

Ideally, each usability study will be a part of a series of studies, where the first study sets the baseline, and all subsequent studies validate the improvements made to the product, and will hopefully measure increased usability in whatever form it was measured originally (task completion rates, satisfaction scores, and so on).

Why? (Finding answers to questions about increasing conversion/decreasing drop-off)

The following are goals we've heard involving the question "Why?":

- "Abandon rates are high."
- "Why do customers download the app and never open it again?"
- "Users register, but never return."
- "Increase the conversion rate of registrations and subscriptions in our app."
- "Our analytics quantitative data says what, but not why."
- "Sales went down when we redesigned the site."
- "Our customer reviews are bad and we want to understand why."

Very often, there is quantitative data available that describes what is going on, but there are no clear insights as to why. While bad usability will probably impact conversions negatively, good usability is only one factor of many that can contribute to increased conversions or decreased drop-off rates. The UX researcher needs to ensure that the stakeholders understand this, in order to set the right expectations.

Understanding the users

Some goals, that customers have listed for understanding their users better, include the following:

- "We want to be more user-centric."
- "Curious how real customers use the app in real life."
- "Does the site engage the user, inspire him to explore?"
- "Acme would like to be a usability company."
- "How can we make the app sticky?"

With the ubiquity of competing applications, companies are turning to user-centered design, to give them an edge over the competition (or so that they at least don't lag behind). Understanding a product's users, what motivates them to use it, and so on, can be studied in usability tests, but should be more of a secondary goal. Usability studies aren't run to get input regarding the customer base of a product, but to determine whether the users find the product easy to use. Knowing who those users are helps to frame the results, but should not be the key goal.

Global suitability

Some goals that we've encountered on the subject of global suitability are as follows:

- "Does our website, which is culturally very European, work outside of Europe?"
- "We want to understand what our Chinese users expect to be present at the very least in an app."

In today's world, the use of digital products is not restricted to a predetermined locality; they can be used across borders and continents. Companies have to take this into consideration and ensure that their products are globally understandable (or are at least understandable in their target markets) and do not breach any local cultural norms.

Comparing design options

The following are some goals that involve comparing design options:

- "We are rebranding our mobile app, and would like to get the users' preference between the different design options."
- "We have three design alternatives and we want to ask our users which design they prefer, and where the usability is the best."

This is a typical goal for a qualitative usability study: "Here are two versions; which do you prefer? And why?" We recommend going into this type of study with an open mind. Study sponsors, launching a comparative study with a clear preference, might end up being disappointed by the results. The users might not validate their choices, or the results might be inconclusive when there is no clear winner.

Comparing to competitors

Customers have listed the following when their goals were competitive analysis:

- "We want an ironclad evaluation of our site search. We would like to use Amazon as a benchmark to compare against."
- "Gain user insight into main competitors, an established provider, and a new startup. Where does our product stand versus the competition in specific markets; what is valued in the competition?"

This is another typical goal for a usability study: measuring a digital interface against the competition's product. It is smart to benchmark where one stands with regard to the competition, and to identify what the competition potentially does better.

Feature validation

The following are some goals related to feature validation that we have heard:

- "Do users understand the features and the terms used?"
- "Do users understand what the trial version comprises, and how they can access it?"
- "What are users looking for in the result set? What information should be displayed here and what shouldn't? What should be on the detail page?"

Feature validation focuses on one or two functions of the product, with the aim of validating the user's recognition of the function, its usefulness, its ease-of-use, potentially missing functions, or other similar goals.

Concept validation

Here are some verbatim goals that we have encountered involving concept validation:

- "Do our customers understand that we are a dropshipper? Does it make them insecure or confuse them?"
- "We have a high-end, tasteful, design-oriented app, targeted at a broad audience. Are users attracted by this? Do they understand the goal of the app?"
- "Our app's purpose is to bring avid readers together. Do our users agree with this statement?"

This can be a valid goal for a usability study, insofar as the concept is reflected in the usage of the product. Asking participants whether they understand the concept behind a given product that they have been asked to test is acceptable because the underlying question is whether the product clearly explains the concept. Asking this question without giving the users the chance to actually use the product is more of a market research study.

Product validation

Some goals that we've encountered on the subject of product validation are as follows:

- "Determine whether it's worth it to continue the effort; is the app useful to users? Would they download it or prefer a website?"
- "The trigger is a relaunch of the app and website. We want to know what users think of the new product."

We don't believe that a usability test is the most appropriate means for finding an answer to the question whether a company should continue to put effort into a product or discontinue it. The usability of the product is only one factor in determining how successful a product is; others may be whether it actually fulfills a need for the users.

What to do next

Some customers use a UX study to get input for planning their next steps, as follows:

- "We have identified 5 features and want to ask customers which features to integrate next."
- "We are looking for direction for our product. We want external input."
- "Understand the users' needs beyond what's in the app today. Are we on the right track with regard to their wants and needs?"

Asking the users what they are looking for in a product can never be wrong. It is even more valuable when the study participants are existing users of the product or similar products, providing feedback that is based on their actual, historical usage of the product being tested.

Predicting future behavior

Other customers will launch a usability study in order to understand the future behavior of their users, as follows:

- "Are people willing to use the service?"
- "Would people recommend the app, or not?"
- "Would people pay for the service?"

We would never accept this as the sole goal of a usability study, because peoples' future behavior is more accurately measured by their past habits than by their predictions. If a person regularly uses a video streaming app on their mobile phone, they are more likely to use a newly introduced video streaming app than someone who has never done so before. Even though this is not a good goal for a usability study, we still include these questions in the study, because they indicate a tendency. If participants can project themselves using a given product or even paying for it, then they probably think it is of interest to them and has value which is relevant feedback.

Classic usability goals

Lastly, we also run usability studies with very traditional goals, such as the following:

- "Are icons enough? Or do we need to include text labels?"
- "There is no commonly used icon for our new feature. Will users understand what it means?"
- "Do users have enough information at hand to choose an option?"
- "Is the navigation intuitive to use? With a given task to complete, do users find the right path within the product?"
- "Do the users notice the filter function?"
- "Is the language used in our product user-friendly, or is it too loaded with jargon?"

Any goal that looks to evaluate how intuitive a product is, is a good goal for a usability study.

The budget

The funds available to finance the usability study can influence the following:

- **The goal**: A small budget might require that the goals are reduced to what can actually be achieved in the frame of that budget.
- **The scope**: The range of tasks to be completed by the participants determines the time required by them, as well as the effort required by the UX researcher, and subsequently, the necessary funding.
- **The test environment**: Development effort might be required to provide working prototypes, or to ensure that the test environment is populated with representative data; devices might have to be shipped to the participants. The cost for these study preparation tasks has to be covered by the available budget, too.
- **The participants**: Elaborate profile requirements for the participants may increase the cost of recruiting suitable candidates. The number of participants is also dependent on the available budget.
- **The study methodology**: Some methodologies are less cost-intensive than others. The available budget can therefore also determine what methodologies are feasible.
- **The deliverables**: Lastly, the budget can determine how much effort is put into producing the deliverables. Instead of a comprehensive written report, the budget might only allow for a summary of the most important findings.

We have encountered projects where the budget was tight, and consequently, we had to reduce the scope or simplify the participant profiles, and so on. The bottom line remains that regardless of your available budget, there is always value in running a usability test.

The scope of the study (the tasks and questions)

The scope is a difficult subject to tackle because stakeholders very often want to use a usability study to cover everything at once, and the UX researcher will have to scale the expectations down to a feasible scope. The scope is constrained by what can reasonably be asked of the participants within the timeframe of the study. A video-based remote usability study will have a different test duration than a survey-based one, for example. The budget also influences the timeframe, and subsequently, the scope.

The goal will determine whether the study's scope should comprise the entire product, only certain functions of it, or even just individual screens. If the goal is to determine the usability status quo of a product, for example, then the scope will encompass the entire product, whereas comparing three design alternatives for a new feature will be restricted to that feature.

The goal will also help to identify which tasks are candidates for the study. A goal of increasing conversion during checkout, for example, will necessarily require that at least one task covers the checkout function. Other tasks may include searching for a suitable product to buy or managing the shopping cart.

The UX researcher should list all of the tasks with an estimated duration and the success criteria for each task. Often, the average task duration can be provided by the stakeholders. Or, the UX researcher may suggest a ballpark. Each task duration can be a rough estimate because there is a lot of variance in the time actually required by study participants to complete a task. The success criteria describe what has to be achieved in order to consider a task successfully completed. For example, if the study participants are testing a checkout journey, the success criteria might be that they complete their purchase, or that they reach the entry of payment information.

If the list of tasks is too extensive, or if the duration is too long, the UX researcher and the study sponsor have to prioritize them, in order to create a shortlist. The goals will help to determine how to prioritize the tasks. For example, tasks in a competitive analysis should comprise the core tasks of the product – the ones that are the main reasons for users using the product. Other ways to prioritize the tasks include sorting them according to frequency of use, or focusing on newly added features or critical tasks that, when done incorrectly, might have severe consequences. Essential tasks, such as logging in or registering, must be a part of the study if they are a prerequisite to using the product under testing. Auxiliary tasks, such as setting preferences, are of secondary priority.

The UX researcher should inform the stakeholders of which benchmark scores they are planning to use, if any, and ask if the study sponsor has any requirements. The benchmark scores increase the time required by a participant completing the study, and should therefore also be listed as a part of the scope. Larger companies might have customized benchmark scores that they use, in order to standardize the results and make them comparable. If this is the case, the UX researcher must understand which questions to ask, how to analyze the responses, and how to derive the score. Examples of some benchmark scores that can be used are covered in the following sections.

Objective benchmark scores

Objective benchmark scores are based on unbiased, factual data that is not influenced by subjective perspectives.

Task completion rate

This score measures the percentage of study participants that are able to complete a given task with the product being tested. It is best used when the product being tested is not a wireframe or an early prototype wherein it is not really possible to complete the task.

Time-on-task

The time-on-task measures the average time required by the study participants that successfully completed the task. It is best used when it is not self-reported by the participant - that is, when either a moderator keeps track of the participant's time-on-task, or the tool being used does it automatically, in order to ensure that it is objective and accurate.

Subjective benchmark scores

Subjective benchmark scores are based on the users' personal perspectives, feelings, and opinions.

Customer Effort Score

The **Customer Effort Score** (CES) measures the average effort a user subjectively felt it took them to complete a task. The score can be expressed as a percentage, or as an index.

Single Ease Question

The **Single Ease Question** (SEQ) score measures the average ease of completing a task, by asking the participants to rate how easy or difficult they subjectively perceived it was to complete. It uses a labeled Likert scale and can be expressed as a percentage or as an index.

Task satisfaction rate

The task satisfaction rate measures the average subjective satisfaction of those study participants that were able to successfully complete the task, or of all participants, regardless of whether they completed the task or not. This is based on asking the participant to rate his satisfaction with the individual task completed or with the product as a whole. The score can be expressed as a percentage or as an index.

Net Promoter Score

The **Net Promoter Score** (**NPS**) is based on one question: How likely it is that the user would recommend the product under testing, rated on a scale of 0-10? It is described as an indicator of customer loyalty, but it is also a measure of customer satisfaction. It is expressed as a percentage, but with a range of `-100%` to `100%`.

System Usability Scale

The **System Usability Scale** (**SUS**) score provides a global measurement of the usability, based on 10 attitude questions and rated using a labeled Likert scale. It is expressed as an index.

USERindex

The USERindex measures the user experience "quick and easy" (analogous to the SUS), but also collects information on metrics such as appeal and satisfaction. It is based on the four dimensions of **Usefulness**, **Satisfaction**, **Ease-of-use** and **Reliability**, and uses 10 attitude questions, rated using a labeled Likert scale. It is expressed as an index.

There is no need (or value) in using all of the benchmark scores listed previously; this would just feel repetitive to the study participant, as some questions may sound similar. Instead, the UX researcher should select those that make the most sense for a given usability study.

Another good point to clarify is the use of scales in rating questions and the order of answers. If you ask ten people their preferences, you will receive ten different opinions. That is why it is good to achieve a consensus before writing the discussion guide/script. We like using 5-scale, labeled rating questions, ordered from the most negative to the most positive, with a neutral element in the middle.

If a stakeholder feels strongly about using a 7-scale, end-labeled rating, with questions ordered from the most positive to the most negative, we would only put in medium effort to discourage them:

I think 5-scale, labeled rating questions are the best.

○ Strongly disagree

○ Somewhat disagree

○ I don't have a strong opinion

○ Somewhat agree

◉ Strongly agree

I think 7-scale, end-labeled rating questions are the best.

1	2	3	4	5	6	7
○	○	○	○	○	○	◉

Strongly agree   Strongly disagree

Example variations of the rating questions

The test environment

While the previous sections were targeted towards ensuring that the study meets the expectations of the study sponsor, this section is about ensuring that the study participants can execute the test as smoothly as possible.

Some of the questions that need to be answered are listed below.

Which are the target devices for the study?

A website might be targeted at both large-screen and small-screen devices; a product might only offer a companion app for iPhones, and so on. These requirements must be documented and taken into consideration when recruiting the participants.

When testing websites, an additional question to ask is which browsers and browser versions are relevant; when testing apps, it's relevant to understand what ratio of smartphone operating systems reflect the actual customer base and should thus be covered. Study sponsors will always say that the app versions for the various smartphone operating systems are identical, but this is not always true. If the versions are significantly different, the UX researcher will have to create separate studies, because the discussion guides/scripts will necessarily be different, too.

What state is the product in?

For a summative usability study, the product being tested may be a live, production version, while a prototype or a test version might be used for a formative usability study.

The development state of the product is important to know, because when a product is not yet publicly available, there may be privacy concerns that need to be addressed. Does the study sponsor require all participants to sign an NDA, for example? We will address how to handle this in `Chapter 3`, *How to Effectively Recruit Participants*.

If the product under testing is to be provided as a test version or on test servers, it is important to understand whether test data is available and whether the test data is representative of live data. For example, if an early prototype only allows for a very specific navigation path that directs the user to buy a television, then it will probably not be relevant to all participants equally if they are not currently looking to buy a TV. It is possible (but not advisable) to run studies with test data that is incomplete (because only mandatory fields have been filled, for example) or not representative (because dummy images have been used instead of real ones, for example), but it is important that the UX researcher is aware of this, in order to prepare the participants. We will look into this in the subsequent chapters on running a study.

It is also prudent to note the version of the product to be tested, and how long it has been live (if it's already in production).

How can the product be accessed?

When a production version is to be tested, one should ask whether it is readily available via a browser or in an app store (and which app stores, in which countries). The UX researcher will need to know the URLs to use, and whether they differ for mobile and desktop.

When a physical device is being tested, it is important to ask whether the participants are required to own that product in order to qualify for participating in the study, or whether the product will be shipped to each participant.

Are special credentials required?

Are credentials required in order to perform the tasks planned for the study? If all participants are to use the same login, can they interfere with each other? Do the study participants have to provide personal data, such as health information or banking details? If the study participants are required to create new accounts, should a list of these be provided to the study sponsor afterward, in order to delete the accounts?

Another aspect to take into consideration is whether the participants will need to have credentials that are only available to residents of the country in which the study is being run. Some government or banking apps/websites, for example, are accessible only to registered residents of the respective countries.

Are there any known bugs?

Especially when testing with early versions, it is possible that there are known bugs or parts of the product that have not yet been implemented. It is better to inform the study participants beforehand that the product is still under development (that not all links will work, that the data displayed may not always be consistent, and so on), rather than letting them run into these issues themselves and potentially negatively influencing their perception of the product.

Any other requirements

The tasks selected to be included in the study might add requirements, such as the necessity to purchase entrance tickets to a conference (in order to test the in-house navigation system) or the need to pick up an order in a store or restaurant. If a purchase is being tested, is dummy credit card data available for the participants to use, or does the study budget include compensation for any costs incurred? If costs will be compensated, the maximum limit has to be set.

The participants

Getting the right participants is key to obtaining relevant results. The following profile requirements should be covered during the kick-off session too.

Demographic requirements

Frequently, the study sponsor can provide the demographics of the participants to be recruited, based on who their typical users are. Having no hard requirements is an acceptable response, because while an educative app for toddlers will only be relevant to parents of young children (and their children, of course), an email application, for example, is very broadly used, and it would probably be difficult to narrow it down to specific demographics.

Some common demographic characteristics that might be relevant include the following:

- Age
- Gender
- Marital status
- Number and age of children
- Ethnicity
- Occupation
- Income
- Location
- Education
- Digital literacy

It is not uncommon to be in a situation where the user groups are known, yet quite vague, such as seniors or millenials. The exact definition of what age ranges those designations encompass can be somewhat different for different people. The UX researcher should ensure that these characteristics are discussed, and that all stakeholders are aligned on the ranges (for example, ages from 18 to 35 years), any distinct values or exclusions (for example, only finance-related occupations), and ratios (for example, 30% male and 70% female participants). It's important to make sure that everyone is on the same page, before starting the recruitment.

Device requirements

The study parameters will also influence the participant profile with regards to device requirements. The following requirements can be derived from the study parameters:

- **Devices**: The participant must own or have access to the device an app or website should be tested on, or the product that is being tested itself.
- **Browsers**: If a website is being tested, the participants may be required to use specific browser versions.
- **Screen size**: Some studies may require a minimum or maximum screen size for the device that the participants will use for testing.
- **Installation of the product under testing**: If the participants are not required to already have the software installed on their devices, then the requirement might be that they agree to install it, in order to be eligible to participate in the study.
- **Installation of the software required to participate in the study**: In remote usability studies, the participants will often be required to install software, such as conferencing software with screen sharing or recording software, depending on the study methodology being used.

Other criteria

The goal will also influence the profile of participants to recruit. For example, if the goal is concept validation, then new users of the product are preferable to existing customers; if the goal is to identify the status quo and determine what is missing, then existing users of the product should be recruited.

Some other possible criteria include the following:

- **Are existing account holders**: Only people who are active customers of the product are eligible to participate in the study.
- **Have used the competition's products within the last 12 months**: For recruitment purposes, the study sponsor will have to provide a list of products that are considered to be competition.
- **Will be buying a new car shortly**: The timeframe should be clearly defined ("shortly" might refer to: in the next month, three months, or six months, for example), as well as whether the study participant must necessarily be the purchaser or the primary decision maker.
- **Are willing to open a new bank account with Acme bank**: Eligible participants are required to have a bank account, but do not need to be existing customers of the bank; they can open an account solely for participating in the study.

- **Shop at Acme retail at least once a month**.
- **Travel mostly for business**: The UX researcher should try to get more detail for this criteria, such as what the required ratio between business and leisure traveling is, whether any type of transportation is eligible (the morning commute on a train might count), and how many business trips the participant should be taking per year.
- **Hold a credit card**: Depending on the goal of the study, it might be relevant to also ask whether the participant is the primary holder of the credit card.
- **Own a car of brand Acme not older than two years**.
- **Are news readers**: It is very important to specify whether paper newspapers are included or excluded, what news sources are relevant, and with what regularity the participants read the news.
- **Interested in buying food locally**.
- **Own pets**: The UX researcher should detail this further, because owning a horse will come with completely different requirements than owning a fish.

The number of participants

Moderated studies are usually qualitative studies, because running a moderated, quantitative study (requiring a larger number of participants) is very cost-intensive. Unmoderated studies can be both quantitative or qualitative, due to their scalability.

We are focusing only on remote, qualitative studies in this book, and for moderated studies, we recommend the following:

- 3-5 participants if you're on a budget or tight deadline, or if you're going to run a series of studies during your development cycle.
- The next step up is 6-8 participants, mostly because you can fit that in a (full) day. You can plan for 8 participants but stop at 5 or 6 if you see that you're not getting any additional feedback.
- 12-15 participants (or more), if the budget and schedule allow it or if more features need to be tested than would fit into a regular session.

For unmoderated studies, we recommend the following:

- 8-12 participants for video-based studies.
- For survey-based studies, larger numbers, such as 15-25 participants, work well, as there is less effort involved in evaluating survey responses, as compared to video feedback.
- For hybrid studies (video- and survey-based), we recommend 12-15 participants.

All figures are per target user group and are merely guidelines.

Even though we have laid it out so cleanly, it is a very contentious topic. Often, a stakeholder may request that a study is executed with more participants, because "more is better, right?" We then defer to Nielsen's study - "After the fifth user, you are wasting your time by observing the same findings repeatedly but not learning much new" (`https://www.nngroup.com/articles/why-you-only-need-to-test-with-5-users/`):

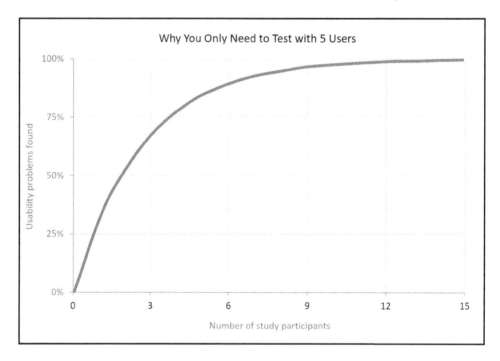

Why you only need to test with 5 users

If they cannot be convinced, we capitulate. There is no harm in running a larger study, other than the increased cost and effort.

The product development methodology may also dictate the number of participants to invite. Agile methodologies advocate a faster, more iterative process, and recommend using as few as 3-5 participants for both moderated and unmoderated studies.

Participant incentives/compensation

If there is a budget to provide an incentive for participants to take part in the study, or compensation for doing so, then this must be agreed upon when planning the study, in order to be able to refer back to it while recruiting.

The study methodology

It is important to understand whether the stakeholders have any expectations regarding the methodology, especially if their preferred method or their comfort zone is in-person usability testing. The UX researcher should take the time to explain the merits of the remote methodologies and why they have been chosen for this specific study. The goals, as well as the available budget, will drive the methodology.

Moderated or unmoderated study

When the goals are vague or it is not possible to pinpoint exactly where to focus the study, a moderated study might be preferable. A moderated study is less rigid than an unmoderated one, because the moderator can react to the individual participants and ask tailored questions, in order to follow up on a particular situation; however, it requires a larger allocation of effort and money.

Video-based and survey-based studies

If the unmoderated option has been chosen, then a further decision to make is whether to run it as a video-based or a survey-based study. Video-based studies are especially useful when it is necessary to see what the participants are doing, or when self-reporting their actions might prove cumbersome, such as in studies focused on path analysis.

If the product under testing involves watching movies (such as a movie streaming service, for example), the UX researcher should inform the stakeholders that due to DRM rights, the recording software will often not show the movie in the video being recorded. We have encountered customers that were not very understanding of this legal requirement, so it is prudent to mention it, and thus ensure that they are aware of it before kicking off the UX study.

Sometimes, a hybrid approach might be the best solution, providing both written and video feedback.

The UX researcher should take the time to walk the stakeholders through the selected study methodology, highlighting its characteristics and explaining why the study best matches the requirements specified by the goal, the product being tested, the available budget, the scope of the study, and the profiles of the participants.

The schedule

The last item to align on is the timeline of the study. Some of the previously listed items will have an influence on the schedule, such as the profile of the participants to recruit. The more specific the profile is, the more time the recruiting may require. The study methodology is also relevant, because setting up the required time slots for moderated studies will probably take longer than running an unmoderated study.

Some other questions that influence the schedule are covered in the following sections.

When will the product be available for testing?

We have kicked off many a study where the product under testing was not yet available even for us to explore because development was ongoing or access still had to be sorted out. The UX researcher cannot start drawing up a discussion guide or a script until they have actually accessed the product and had the opportunity to explore its features for themselves. In this case, the start of the study is dynamic, and depends on when access to the product under testing will be possible. If all of the stakeholders understand this, it should not pose a problem.

Are there any hard deadlines?

The goal of the usability study may be to get a baseline usability benchmark before the product goes live. The timing of the product launch will thus be a factor when planning the schedule, especially if any usability issues found should be fixed before going live. Another hard deadline may be an upcoming management presentation, where the results of the study are part of the agenda. The UX researcher should ask this question in order to understand and cater for any constraints on the schedule.

Are there any update cycles that need to be taken into consideration?

Many products are on a regular update cycle, which means that bug fixes, and also new features, are rolled out at regular intervals. In order to ensure that the version used during the study is stable, the UX researcher needs to know when updates are planned, and ideally, run the study between these update cycles. It might also be an option to skip an update cycle. In either case, it is pertinent to address this issue and agree on how to deal with it.

Do the participants need to be equipped with physical devices?

If the product under testing needs to be shipped to the participants, the coordination of the delivery, the delivery times to the various destinations, and any potential delays due to customs checks, have to be taken into account. We have also run into delays when the plugs of the devices being shipped were local to the country manufacturing them, while the participants they were being shipped to lived in countries with other standards for plugs and sockets. Either the participants are then asked to buy adapters, or the study sponsor sends them out to all participants.

What time of year is the study planned for?

When planning studies, it is prudent to avoid the typical holiday seasons in the various locations where participants are being recruited, because it is harder to find participants during vacation time; people are more distracted by year-end closing (and potentially religious holidays) in early December, for example. This makes recruitment more difficult, and may also result in a higher risk of no-shows, with subsequent delays in the study schedule.

Is a pilot run with participants/stakeholders necessary?

A pilot run should be part of the study setup. In a pilot run, the study is executed with a small set of participants, which may be stakeholders or people that match the required profile. The aim is to validate that the discussion guide/script is ready to be used in the actual study, or else to identify how to improve it.

A pilot run influences the schedule because it needs to be planned and executed, and also because it might require an update to the discussion guide/script and subsequent approval by the stakeholders. In unmoderated studies, the UX researcher may run through the survey by themselves, instead of inviting participants or stakeholders to do so, reducing the required time.

Is external approval required?

Most studies do not require formal external approval, but UX studies that are conducted using regulated devices, such as medical devices, may require additional approval and involve further restrictions. Details of such approvals are outside of the scope of this book.

Do external factors impose a schedule on the UX study?

Some studies might require that they are executed in a very specific time window. An app for keeping track of the Wimbledon Championship scores will be best tested during the duration of the tournament, and an app to navigate conference halls can only be tested when the conference is ongoing.

Taking all of this into account, the UX researcher should provide a schedule that includes dates for when the following should occur:

- UX researcher provides study framework documentation
- Stakeholders sign off on study framework
- UX researcher provides a first draft of the discussion guide/script
- Stakeholders provide feedback for discussion guide/script
- UX researcher provides the final version of the discussion guide/script
- UX researcher executes a pilot run

- UX researcher runs the study
- UX researcher provides results of the study

The deliverables

The following sections will cover the typical deliverables in a remote usability study.

Study framework for sign off

The study framework is a summary of everything that we've covered in this chapter thus far. We have added a template for a checklist in the appendix, which can be used to ensure that all of the relevant questions have been asked, and the responses duly documented. Ideally, all stakeholders will sign off on the framework, in order to kick off the study.

Participant screener

Based on the participant profile, the UX researcher will develop a screener to recruit the right people. This is also a deliverable of the study, which we will discuss in more detail in the following chapter.

Discussion guide/script

The actual study will be led by either a discussion guide (for moderated studies) or a script (for unmoderated studies). Both are deliverables that the UX researcher has to develop as a part of the study. We will cover these in subsequent chapters.

At this point, it is important to set expectations on how many review iterations will be included. Ideally, the UX researcher will present a first draft of the discussion guide or script to the stakeholders, and they will review it and provide their feedback. The UX researcher will then incorporate the feedback, in order to produce the final version that will be used in the study. Unfortunately, there are situations where multiple iterations are requested. We have run into this when the stakeholders are numerous and not fully aligned. In these constellations, the UX researcher is well advised to set the maximum number of review iterations at kick-off as multiple, unplanned iterations of the disussion guide (or script) will negatively impact the study schedule.

Report

The UX researcher should clarify the expectations with regards to how the results will be communicated, as follows:

- **Format**: We recommend wrapping up a usability study with a written report because it avoids having to repeat the results (and potentially not get the details right) if new stakeholders join later, and also makes the results available for subsequent studies to compare to. Some study sponsors might not want to spend effort on a written report, however, especially if the scope of the study is not very large. In that case, they might request a simple discussion of the main findings.
- **Language**: In globally distributed studies, where the study language might not be the language of the study sponsor, it is germane to align on the language the report is expected to be written in.
- **Recommendations**: The raw results of a usability study might provide information about potential usability issues, but they do not, on their own, provide recommendations on their resolution. This is where the expertise of the UX researcher comes in. UX researchers interpret the raw results, identify the underlying issues, and suggest improvements that should be a part of the report. When the stakeholders or study sponsors are UX researchers themselves, they might prefer to receive the raw study results and make their own inferences.
- **Topline report:** A topline report is often provided 24 hours after the last session, in a moderated study.

Next steps

We like to end a meeting with a quick rundown of the agreed timeline, followed by a short recap of the next steps. After a kick-off session, the typical next step is to send out the study framework for approval. The UX researcher should use this opportunity to identify who the main contacts for the study will be, and thus, who will receive the deliverables of the study.

Summary

Properly planning a study involves documenting all of the aspects that will influence its execution; this ensures that all of the stakeholders are on the same page, and are in agreement on how to run the study. The goal of the study influences nearly every aspect of it and should be given appropriate consideration.

Recruiting participants is a significant effort in preparing a study, and merits its own chapter. This topic will, therefore, be covered in the following chapter.

3
How to Effectively Recruit Participants

In Chapter 2, *What Not to Forget When Planning Your Study*, we focused on the overall planning of a study. An important aspect of planning a study is finding suitable candidates and having them sign up for the study.

In this chapter, we will cover the different aspects of recruiting, including the following:

- The importance of profiling participants that represent the target users
- Recruiting specific target user groups, such as minors or subject matter experts
- The advantages and disadvantages of self-recruiting, versus using a third-party recruiting source
- How to screen and set expectations
- Compensation

An informed approach to recruiting participants is yet another crucial factor in ensuring the success of the study.

Who to recruit

The goal of any usability study is to understand whether the target users of the product are able to use it with ease, and whether they would like to use the product in the future and will recommend it to others.

Participants whose profiles are the most similar to the target users will therefore provide the most relevant feedback. Imagine running a study on a retail website that targets people who are 50 years of age and older. Feedback from millennials may not be very relevant, since younger people interact with technology differently than older people do. For instance, millennials might not comment on the font size, color contrast, and readability of the site, even though these are likely pain points for some older users.

Or, imagine a product used by nurses to monitor patients in the intensive care unit of a hospital. If the study participants don't have the relevant work experience, they will be hard-pressed to provide meaningful insights into the ease of using the product.

A company that wants to roll out an E-commerce site in a different country should plan to use local study participants in order to understand the ease-of-use and the users' expectations, and to confirm that the site is localized appropriately in order to ensure user engagement. Users in Japan, the US, the UK, and Brazil, may all have different expectations.

As mentioned in the previous chapter, target user profiles can be broad and vague, including groups like seniors or millenials. In order to recruit a representative set of participants, however, the UX researcher and the stakeholders must agree upon a more specific definition. For instance, the age range for seniors must be agreed upon. This alignment will ensure that the screener effort will be efficient. We will cover the screener later in this chapter.

Multiple target user groups

Many products are used by a wide range of users. This trend will only continue, as we build an increasingly digital world. If the product usage and expectations are significantly different among users, it makes sense to consider these as different user groups.

In the example of a global website, Japanese and British users are likely two distinct target user groups. Existing and novice users of a product comprise another example of distinct user groups; at least, they should be considered distinct when running a study, in order to understand whether user behaviors and expectations are different.

Many UX professionals use personas to describe the different target user groups. A persona is a description of a fictitious person that represents a target user of the product. Persona descriptions give this fictitious person human attributes, such as a name, age, profession, and hobbies. Products typically have one to three primary personas, and possibly a few secondary personas.

Personas list attributes that may not be directly relevant to the use of the product. Target user descriptions, on the other hand, focus on attributes that are only relevant to the use of the product. In this book, we will refrain from using personas, or the term persona, and will instead favor "target users" or "target user groups."

When the target user (almost) doesn't exist

It is sometimes difficult to find participants that fit the target user profile.

Finding existing users of an app that was recently launched may be difficult; imagine a service that was launched just days ago, and only has a subscriber base of 50 people. Unless it is possible to target precisely that group of users, it will be very challenging to find existing users within a broader community. In some cases, it makes sense to identify a group of study participants that agree to use the product for a period of time before participating in the study, thereby artificially creating existing users.

User profiles can be so specific that they become an obstacle to recruitment. A study sponsor once requested study participants who were male, between 33 and 37 years old, divorced with children, and earning less than a certain (low) wage. Presumably, some data had identified this profile as a distinct buyer group. This profile was so restrictive, however, that a lot of effort and time was spent trying to find matching participants. One can assume that the divorced status, requirement to have children and earning a lower wage are all indicators of someone who doesn't have a lot of disposable income. As a result, a broader profile focusing on the more relevant criteria such as age and lack of disposable income might have sufficed.

Recruiting for specific target user groups

Recruiting participants from the general consumer population can be easy or difficult, depending on the specific demographic requirements, as mentioned previously. Some products are used by specific groups of users, such as minors, seniors, certain professionals, or people with disabilities. There may be specific challenges in running studies within these groups.

Minors

When running remote studies with children, unmoderated studies are often the better choice, especially with younger children. Products aimed at children often include a gamification component to engage the child, such as leveling up and unlocking prizes. Unlocking rewards typically requires extended usage of the product, and such studies often run over a period of a week or two.

Since the children are minors, their parents are required to sign up for the study. They play an active part in the study, and are prompted to get direct feedback from the child, observe and report on the child's behavior, and provide their own feedback on the product throughout the study.

Recruiting sets of parents and children that will commit to participating for the entire duration of the study can be challenging.

Seniors

The main challenge when recruiting seniors for usability studies is that many don't feel as comfortable with technology as younger age groups do (`http://www.pewinternet.org/2017/05/17/technology-use-among-seniors/`). They may be intimidated by the prospect of participating in a UX study during which they need to use technology, as they may dread that they will fail at the tasks.

If seniors are one of the target user groups, it is definitely beneficial to include them in usability testing. As a group, seniors use technology quite differently compared to younger age groups and they have different needs. Some struggle with reduced motor skills or reduced vision, which can make it harder to manipulate a mouse or use a touchscreen.

People with disabilities

There is an increasing interest in not only complying with accessibility standards, but also understanding, measuring, and improving the user experience for those that use assistive tools or have certain conditions that benefit from alternative ways of interacting with products.

There is a wide range of types of disabilities, including visual, hearing, motor skills, and cognitive impairments, and the severity of the conditions can vary greatly. Visual impairments, for instance, can range from total blindness to mild color blindness. Thus, a wide range of assistive tools is available to help with different types of impairments. The assistive tool that is used will directly impact the user's experience.

In order to effectively recruit for and run studies with people with disabilities, the UX researcher must have sufficient knowledge of the topic, or else involve an accessibility specialist. In-depth coverage of this topic is outside of the scope of this book.

Subject matter experts

Recruiting subject matter experts can be challenging. Subject matter experts, such as surgeons, fund managers, architects, farmers, or restaurant chefs, usually have busy schedules, limiting the time that they have available for participating in UX studies.

Many studies provide some form of financial compensation as an incentive. However, subject matter experts in higher paying jobs are often not swayed by compensation as an incentive. They will typically participate in a study out of personal or professional interests, and often respond well to charity donations as appreciation for their participation.

Remote studies (as compared to in-person studies) can be advantageous, since the busy participant does not need to spend time traveling to a facility. This is especially valuable for studies involving participants in rural areas or in specific industries; for instance, when running a study on the usability of farming or oil drilling equipment. Unmoderated studies offer the additional benefit that the participant does not need to commit to a particular time slot.

Who is really participating in your study?

A study is an artificial construct that aims to mimic real life as closely as possible, in order to gather data. Study participants are an artificially created group that represents the larger user population as best as possible. Yet, this artificially constructed group will not perfectly reflect a random subset of the user population.

Think about what would happen if you were to stand at the entrance of a store or a subway station and ask people if they wanted to take part in a survey. Some people won't have time, others won't trust it, and others don't like to talk about their opinions. Those that are responsive either have time, love to talk, or are interested in the reward (or a combination thereof). Your survey will get input from a skewed subset of all passersby.

That is the reality of many consumer-oriented studies. We aim to get as close to the real user profile as possible, knowing that the findings will represent the total user population well enough, but not perfectly.

How to find participants

The UX researcher can either do the recruiting themselves or involve a third party. The advantages and disadvantages of both approaches are described in the following sections.

Self-recruiting

The self-recruiting UX researcher can find participants through different means, including asking coworkers and friends and family of coworkers to participate, using advertisements or identifying existing customers that are willing to provide feedback.

Coworkers

Coworkers are one of the most easily accessible and cheapest groups of participants. If coworkers are co-located, in-person testing may be an option. Yet, many companies have geographically distributed offices, and reaching folks across the company thus requires the use of remote methodologies.

The main disadvantage of recruiting coworkers is the higher likelihood that they are biased; they may have worked on the product themselves, they may know someone who does, or they may already have heard good or bad feedback about the product from others. This may influence their own feedback on the product. To find the least biased coworkers, supporting departments, such as accounting and operations, are often targeted.

Friends and family

Recruiting the friends and family of coworkers reduces bias, since there is a level of separation between the UX researcher and the participant. However, it introduces a dependency, as well, since coworkers need to actively recruit their friends and family, and could end up being a bottleneck in getting participants connected with the originator of the request.

When approaching coworkers with a request, we recommend providing a written paragraph that explains what the study is about and adding contact information. The written information can easily be passed on to interested parties, who can then reach out to the contact person directly.

Note that the study setup needs to be more formal with this group than with coworkers. As they are further removed from the source, there is less knowledge about the study and its goal. Informing the participants adequately becomes more important. Overall, this is a low-effort recruiting method, and can be a great compromise.

Recruiting Ads

Requests for participants can be shared through a number of channels including the company blog or newsletter, sites such as Facebook, Craigslist, LinkedIn groups and so on. Participants likely will not be connected to the company, and proper communication and screening will be required. We will further discuss communication later in this chapter.

Customers

There are a number of ways to tap into your customer base to get user feedback. Engaging customers can be very helpful when the product under testing requires specific domain knowledge. Consider a product that is used by the human resources department, to manage the hiring process from posting a job description to offering a position to a candidate. Someone with no training in the subject matter will probably not know how to use the tool effectively. Their feedback would largely be meaningless.

One of the ways to identify possible participants is to have customer support ask customers who call in if they want to participate in a study. Another option is to ask the customer relationship manager of your company to approach the customer with the request. On a number of occasions, we have had to deal with internal colleagues that are reluctant to do so, as they view asking for product feedback as showing a weakness.

Our view is that it can be immensely useful to get feedback from existing customers, and we absolutely recommend attempting it.

Self-recruiting is often a convenient way to find study participants but they may not be fully representative of the target users. An alternative to self-recruiting is to use a third-party panel company.

Panel companies

If the UX researcher does not have the time or man power to recruit participants themselves, and the budget is available, a third-party panel company can be a good option.

Panel companies are companies that have large databases of potential users with diverse profiles. People sign up to be part of a panel and participate in surveys for a nominal compensation. Panel companies can be a great way to find specific profiles or participants that are not biased. An online search for 'panel companies' yields links to individual companies as well as directories.

However, panel companies are not the magical answer to all problems, and being successful when collaborating with panel companies requires some thought and work to ensure that the right types of participants are recruited and expectations are clearly communicated.

Representations of target users

Some panel companies are large and have a broad reach, while others address niche markets. The UX researcher should confirm that the panel company has a strong foothold in the targeted market or space, or has relationships with partners in areas where they themselves are not well represented. The applies both to the types of target users and their geographic locations.

Expectations

When engaging with a panel company, make sure that you understand the agreement on the table, and read the fine print. Some things to consider are as follows:

- Is the agreement set up to deliver a certain number of completed responses or only started responses?
- What is the resolution when not enough participants are found within a predefined timeframe?
- How are fraudulent submissions handled?

While overhead should be minimal as compared to self-recruiting, the time and cost can vary greatly.

Screening the participants

At the start of this chapter, we stressed that using participants that resemble the target user as closely as possible will yield the most insightful user feedback. To identify the right participants, the candidates must be screened for those profile requirements.

When working with a panel company, it is important to clearly communicate the profile requirements and list them in order of importance, especially when the profiles are challenging to recruit for. The UX researcher should review the screener before the panel company starts recruitment.

Screener methods

Screeners can be conducted over the phone or online, using a survey. Phone screeners are more personal, as there is direct person-to-person interaction. It is also a slow and labor- and time-intensive process. A survey is impersonal, but can be created quickly and sent out to a large number of people with ease. Costs may vary depending on the platform used, but they are typically much lower than phone screeners.

Proponents of phone screeners claim that the added level of personal interaction results in higher participation and completion rates. We suggest that phone screeners may be considered for remote moderated studies, since moderated studies require an increased commitment, and no-shows can be more costly. For an unmoderated study, recruiting additional participants is not as resource-intensive, so it may be more economical to use the survey method and over-invite, in order to counterbalance the dropouts.

The number of participants

Not all participants that are screened and agree to participate in the study will end up participating. As a rule of thumb, we recommend over-recruiting by 30%. This number can vary, depending on the recruiting method, the study method, the type of study, and the available budget.

Challenges

The main challenge with the screener creation is that when demographic requirements lack definition, the survey questions lack precision.

Imagine, for instance, that the stakeholder wants to use existing users of the product to gauge user perception and feedback of a redesign versus the current experience. The concept of an existing user is easy to understand, but should be further refined into actual requirements. Existing users are defined by the frequency of use, the recency of use, or both. This definition will change based on the product; a product that is not used very often, such as an app to pay monthly bills, might consider existing users to be those that use the product once a month. An email app, on the other hand, might not consider someone that uses the app once a month as a frequent enough user. It is important to take recency into account; a user who last used an app nine months ago may not remember their experience well enough to provide insightful comparative feedback. Screening for use, therefore, needs to include a question about frequency of use, as well as how often the product is used over a period of time.

Imagine that, for the product being tested, an existing user typically uses the product a few times per week, and will have done so for at least the last few months. The first screener question may ask the following:

- How often do you use this product?
  - Once a year, or less often
  - A few times a year
  - Once a month
  - Once a week
  - Several times a week
  - Once a day
  - Multiple times a day

For those that qualify based on this question (those that selected "Several times a week" or more often), a follow-up question can be asked to determine the elapsed time of use, as follows:

- How long have you been using this product?
  - A year, or longer
  - Between 6 and 12 months
  - Between 3 and 6 months
  - Less than 3 months

Another example is a target user that is a car enthusiast. It is important to understand whether this person is a fan of old cars, new cars, fast cars, race cars, and so on. In addition, the concept of an enthusiast must be defined. Should this person own such a car, actively be restoring a car, not own the car but be willing enough to own one that they buy car magazines, or should they simply be interested in such cars? These are very different backgrounds, which may impact the usefulness of feedback that the participants can provide.

The UX researcher must bring up this discussion early in the process and request sign-offs from stakeholders on the details before starting the screening. If this is not discussed early on, screening may have to be restarted because there are discrepancies between the stakeholders' expectations of the participants and the actual screened group.

The screener questionnaire should be objective, clear, and deal with sensitive questions appropriately. Best practices for proper survey question writing are covered in Chapter 6, *Running a Remote Unmoderated Study with a Survey*.

Informing the participants

When attracting potential participants for a study, it is important to explain the expectations upfront. If expectations are clearly set at the start, a larger number of participants will be inclined to complete the study.

Time commitments

Potential participants need to understand how much time they will spend on the overall study, and how that time will be spent. For instance:

- Will there be one single session, or multiple smaller sessions? What is the duration of a session? If there are multiple sessions, what is the total duration? For instance, if the study requires three sessions, will these sessions occur over the course of a week, two weeks, or one month?
- How much flexibility is there in the timeframe for completion, once the participant is notified that the session can be started? Does each session need to be completed within an hour or a day?

Not only is it important to explain the time commitments ahead of the study, it is equally important to communicate any delays during the study, should they occur. It is important to minimize shifts in the schedule as much as possible, as these may result in participants withdrawing from the study.

Location

Informing the participants about the location of the study is just as important. Does the participant need to visit a location, or can they join the study from their home? It is possible for remote studies to involve a trip to a location outside of the home. As brick-and-mortar outfits continue to increase their digital experiences, participants may, for instance, be asked to order an item using a website or an app, and then visit a physical location to pick up the item.

Online versus offline

Participants must understand whether they will complete the session on their own which is typical for remote, unmoderated studies (offline), or if they will interact with someone remotely (online). If online interaction is required, it is important to explain what this interaction consists of.

In remote moderated studies, the participant may be interacting online with a technical person, ahead of the actual session. This person is responsible for helping the participant set up their environment for the study and troubleshooting in case of any issues. During the session, the participants will interact with a moderator, and the participant is expected to share their screen and potentially allow webcam sharing. Participants may be concerned by screen sharing, especially since sessions are recorded. Financial and medical products, for instance, will probably require the user to enter or view private data. Some participants may decline to participate because they have privacy concerns, or simply because they don't like the idea of being observed in such a direct manner.

Devices and tools

Be clear upfront about the devices and tools that the participant will need to use, and who will supply them. It is reasonable to expect that the participant has access to common devices, such as a desktop computer, a mobile phone, or a tablet. Some devices may not be as ubiquitous, such as smart appliances, or cars of a certain make, model, and year. Finding participants that own these products may be difficult. If a product is not commonplace but can be shipped easily, sending the device to the participant may be an option. For devices that are still under development, shipping it to the participants beforehand is necessary, as they are not available for purchase yet.

Similarly, participants can be expected to have access to common tools, such as a text editor or publicly available apps or websites. Any developmental versions of apps or specific recording tools will need to be supplied.

Expectations

It is expected that participants that commit to participating in the study complete the study, follow the instructions, do their best in completing the tasks, and give feedback that is honest and reflects their perceptions and opinions. Those expectations should be communicated to the participants.

In many studies, it is important not to share with the possible participants who commissioned the study in order to avoid participant bias. This is especially important in competitive studies.

If participants are interacting with an early prototype they may realize which brand they are testing a product for. The study sponsor may require them to sign a confidentiality agreement or non-disclosure agreement (NDA). Even when testing live products, the participants may be asked to keep the study information confidential – when the tasks and questions could potentially lead to an understanding of a future marketing or business decision, for example.

An NDA is, "A legally enforceable contract that creates a confidential relationship between a person who holds some kind of trade secret and a person to whom the secret will be disclosed" (`https://www.rocketlawyer.com/article/nda-101:-what-is-a-non-disclosure-agreement.rl`). An NDA can be emailed to the study participants as a prerequisite for taking part in the study. An electronic signature using an eSign service usually suffices.

Compensation

Compensation can take on a number of forms. These can be categorized as monetary and non-monetary.

Monetary compensation

Monetary compensation includes cash and gift cards that can easily be delivered online.

Cash

Cash is the most direct form of compensation. Panel companies compensate their panelists with cash. During the sign-up process with a panel company, the panelist sets up the payment method – usually an online option. This makes it easy to distribute the payments.

Gift cards

Gift cards for large online retailers or ubiquitous establishments are almost as good as cash, and can be emailed to participants. Examples are Amazon or Starbucks in the United States and other countries, Rakuten in Japan, or Tesco in the UK and Ireland. They are a good option when payment information is not available; for instance, when recruiting through your network or ads.

Donations

As mentioned earlier in this chapter, subject matter experts in higher-paying jobs such as surgeons are challenging to recruit. While their compensation can be calculated based on their typical hourly rate, we have found that they are more likely to respond to a charity donation on their behalf. Provide these participants with a short list of organizations to choose from.

Non-monetary compensation

Non-monetary methods include lottery drawings, promotional items, and sheer gratitude.

Lottery drawings

Lottery drawings can be an attractive option, because they are inexpensive. However, before deciding to use a lottery drawing, check that they are legal in the area you are recruiting participants from. In the past, we have used lottery drawings with the restriction that participants had to supply their contact info, had to be informed of when the drawing was to be held and be notified of who the winner was (via email).

Promotional items

Promotional items can be a good way to compensate participants that have a relationship with the company. Note, however, that remote studies require the promotional items to be shipped out. This requires that participants' addresses are collected and that items are packaged up adequately and taken to the post office. Fragile items (such as mugs) may present a packaging challenge, and larger items may be expensive to ship. An electronic gift card is often a more efficient and cheaper alternative.

Sheer gratitude

There may be times when there is no budget to compensate your participants. At other times, a company's gifting policy may not allow compensation.

When in this position, all is not lost. Some general characteristics of human behavior that work in your favor are as follows:

- **Many people like to help, when asked**: People like feeling useful, and find it rewarding to contribute.

- **People like to have their voices heard**: Consumers of products have ideas and gripes. Many love to voice their feedback, and often feel that there is no easy way to do so. Approaching potential participants and explicitly telling them that you want to hear what they have to say can be a great way to engage people. Do make sure to phrase the request in such a way that there is no expectation that all comments and suggestions will actually make it into a future product.
- **People respond well to polite and thankful interaction**: As participants complete the session, "please" and "thank you" can go a long way.

How much is the right amount?

It may be difficult to gauge how much a participant should be compensated. Compensation is directly related to the ease of finding participants and the complexity of what is asked of them.

The ease of finding participants depends on a number of things that we have previously discussed in this chapter, including how specific the target group requirements are and the effort the participants need to commit to. Finding participants for a short survey that covers online retail behavior is much easier than finding participants for a moderated study using a medical device.

In general, moderated studies require a substantially larger compensation than online surveys, because the real-time moderated interaction requires a larger commitment; participants must be available at a certain day and time, and have to share their screen and webcam.

When to provide compensation

The question here is whether to provide compensation only after a successfully completed session, or to also provide compensation when a participant does not complete the session. Studies that must adhere to certain regulations, such as studies with medical devices, follow compensation rules as dictated by the regulations.

For all other studies, there are no hard compensation rules. Here's where common sense and courtesy (should) prevail. If a remote moderated study participant put reasonable effort into setting up their system to participate, the participant should be compensated for their effort, even if the session could not take place. Take, for example, a remote moderated study with participants that are not tech-savvy. Participants are expected to download a tool and make sure that their camera is running. If the participant is provided with clear instructions and hands-on tech help, yet still cannot get their system working, this participant should be compensated for their effort.

Consider a 15-minute survey, on the other hand. A given participant completed the survey, but the system log shows that the participant spent less than 2 minutes on it, and the answers show that the participant gave the questions little or no thought. The rating questions are all answered the same way or follow a pattern, and the open-ended feedback answers list "n/a" instead of insightful commentary, for example. While this participant completed the session, they did not fulfill the expectations for providing honest and clear feedback to the best of their ability. This participant can be disqualified, and hence, not receive payment.

Deciding where to draw the line between reasonable effort and fraudulent behavior can be tricky. It is important to keep in mind that not all participants are created equal, and that every study will usually have a few participants that provide considerably less valuable information than others, despite showing reasonable effort. Use your best judgment.

Extra costs

Certain studies will require the participant to pay out of pocket; for instance, when tasks include ordering food or goods online. It should be made clear to participants whether the items will be reimbursed, and up to what price limit. Always make sure to be very clear about the upper limit, and ensure that it is expressed in the local currency of the participant or the product (if this differs). It is equally important to communicate what type of proof the participant must provide in order to be reimbursed, when the deadline for providing that proof is, and when they can expect their reimbursement.

Next steps

So far, we've covered who to recruit, how to find participants, and what to inform them about. These steps will yield a list of potential study participants. Note that all of the information about the participants so far has been self-reported by the participant, and their claims have not been confirmed.

Re-screening participants

Re-screening by using means other than self-reporting may be desirable in some cases. It can be a tricky situation, because of both feasibility and the risk of damaging the rapport with the participants.

Re-screening on key profile aspects may not work if they are linked to habits or interests. If a key profile attribute is that coffee lovers drink more than four cups of coffee a day, on average, it is impossible to follow each of these participants as they go about their daily lives, in order to count the number of cups of coffee they consume.

If, on the other hand, participants must be existing customers of a particular utility provider, a copy of a statement can be requested as proof. Asking for such private information after a possible participant has self-reported this information may be perceived as a lack of trust, however, which will negatively impact the relationship. It is important to find the right balance between asking for confidential information and building trust.

Unfortunately, enough potential participants misrepresent themselves in screeners that re-screening is a prudent step to take. Having participants that don't fit the target profile participate in a study may reduce the sponsor's confidence in the results, as well as in the UX researcher's ability to provide relevant insights. We suggest re-screening in situations where it might be beneficial. Proper messaging when requesting the follow-up information can limit negative impressions from participants.

One re-screening factor that is crucial to the study is language proficiency. Study participants must be proficient and able to communicate their thoughts and impressions clearly in the language of the study. While replying to a screener in a given language might seem like an implied acknowledgment of proficiency in that language, that is not always the case. And, having a participant in a moderated study that barely speaks the language but kindly invited a translator to join him is not a great experience (yes, you guessed it – this happened to us).

To avoid these situations, especially in remote moderated studies with observers, a quick, post-screener phone call is helpful. It only takes a few minutes to ascertain their suitability, and this call can be used to build rapport or communicate the next steps.

Building a database for future recruiting

Once you have put all of this effort into recruiting and screening potential participants, consider creating a database for future use. Be sure to check your local privacy laws before embarking on such endeavor. In order for this effort to be useful in the future, document the following:

- The answers to the screener questions, for every participant that answered the questions properly and could be a viable candidate in the future.

- The following metadata:
    - The date of screening is important, since information goes stale. Some information becomes stale faster than other information. The mobile device make and model might change faster than pet ownership, for example.
    - The source where you found the person.
    - Any compensation expectations that were shared.
    - The type of study they were screened for.

- If the person participated in a study, also consider recording the following:
    - Whether they completed the study per the expectations; for example, if they showed up on time, completed the study, and so on.
    - How valuable their feedback was and whether they are a good communicator.
    - How likely you would be to have them participate again in the future.

Summary

Building a group of participants for a study requires effort. The more conscientious one is about who to recruit, how to recruit, and how to inform the participants properly, the higher the chances are that the participants will show up and provide relevant feedback.

Participation is crucial in every methodology, but it perhaps has the biggest ramifications in remote moderated studies. The next chapter will provide in-depth information on how to run remote moderated studies.

Running a Remote Moderated Study

4

As we discussed in Chapter 1, *Why Everyone Should Run Remote Usability Studies*, in a remote moderated usability study, the UX researcher and the study participant are both present and connected, but they are not in the same location.

Moderated studies use the internet and collaborative software, so the UX researcher can watch the participant interact with the product being tested and can see their facial expressions. Real-time moderation makes it possible to ask additional questions, based on what is observed as the participant.

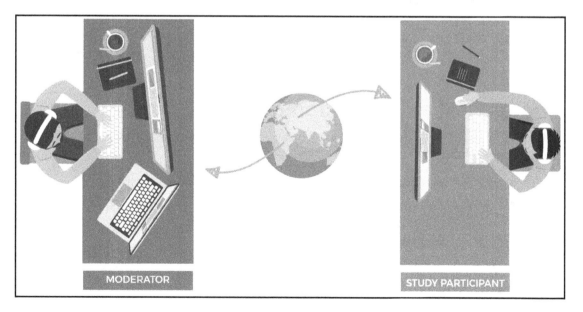

Remote moderated study

Stakeholders that are familiar with in-person studies may see remote moderated studies as a justifiable compromise, as compared to in-person testing, because of the ability to observe, ask follow-up questions, and include participants from different geographies, without incurring additional costs.

Compared to unmoderated testing, remote moderated testing requires considerably more effort in recruiting, scheduling and managing participants and moderating the sessions. The installation and use of moderating software on the participant side can be a challenge, as well.

The major efforts involved in remote moderated studies are as follows:

- Recruiting and managing participants
- Writing a discussion guide
- Pre-session setup
- Running sessions
- Analyzing the data and writing the reports

Discussion guide

The moderator creates a discussion guide based on their conversations with the stakeholders concerning the study's goals. The moderator then uses the discussion guide to structure the session, and to make sure that he covers all of the tasks with each participant.

Anatomy of a discussion guide

A discussion guide has different sections. The approximate times per section are based on a one-hour session duration, as follows:

- Introduction (5 minutes)
- Warm-up (5 minutes)
- Tasks (40 minutes)
- Post-session questions (5 minutes)
- Wrap-up (5 minutes)

Sample discussion guides are provided in the appendix.

Introduction

The introduction is used to set the stage and tone for the session, and for the moderator to build rapport with the study participant. The moderator performs the following:

- Introduces himself
- Thanks the participant for participating in the study
- Describes what will happen in the session
- Stresses that the goal is to get honest user feedback
- Explains that there are no right or wrong answers
- Explains the think-aloud method
- If the product being tested is a prototype, explains its limitations
- Informs the participant of the following:
    - The session will be recorded
    - Observers are present in the background (if applicable)
    - Consent is needed to record the session
- Engages in small talk to build rapport (optional)

Thinking aloud refers to the participants speaking out loud as to what they are thinking as they complete each task. This method originated in cognitive psychology and has been around for a few decades. There is some interesting research on the topic, including this research paper by Charters (`https://brock.scholarsportal.info/journals/brocked/home/article/download/38/38`). It references resources that state that think-aloud data is a thoroughly reliable method to get insights into the thoughts and impressions a user has. Throughout the session, the moderator may need to remind the participant to continue thinking aloud.

Warm-up

The warm-up is used to ease into the session as participants are sometimes nervous at the start of the session. First-time participants, in particular, may not know what to expect. UX studies often require collecting some information on the participant, their background, and prior interactions with the product (or a similar product). Such background questions comprise an excellent warm-up exercise.

If the study covers a retail website, for instance, suitable warm-up questions would be as follows:

- "Do you shop for clothing for yourself only or for a household?"
- "How often do you shop online? How often do you go to a store?"

- "When would you shop online versus at a store?"
- "When shopping online, what type of device do you use most often (for example, a computer or mobile phone), and why?"

An alternative warm-up option is for the participant to complete a simple task. Ideally, this task will be related to the study. The results from this task may or may not be used in the actual analysis.

Tasks

This is the core part of the session. Participants are asked to complete a number of tasks and answer follow-up questions after each task.

How many tasks and questions?

It is not easy to suggest a right number of tasks and questions, since tasks can vary greatly in scope and complexity, and those factors, in turn, determine the time required to complete the task. In addition, some questions yield short answers, while others yield long answers, taking more time to answer. Four to seven tasks is a good general number, and an experienced UX researcher will have a sense of the right length of the discussion guide based on the session duration.

Not all participants are equal, either; some are slower than others in completing tasks and verbalizing their thoughts. Hence, some sessions will be shorter than others. In a six-participant study with a discussion guide that is optimized towards the one-hour session duration, it is not unusual to have the majority of participants complete all tasks in about an hour, while one participant finishes in 40 minutes and another needs to be cut off after one hour and 20 minutes.

Before starting the sessions, the UX researcher must discuss whether breadth or depth is more important with the study sponsor and stakeholders. When a session looks like it is going to run long because feedback on a particular task is taking longer (and is relevant), the UX researcher must know whether to investigate and encourage the deeper discussion (perhaps at the expense of some later tasks) or to move on to the next task, so that all tasks can be addressed by each participant.

It is also important to define upfront when participants who are not able to complete a task will be told to discontinue the efforts. If the participant struggles, they may spend precious time that could be used more wisely. They can, in addition, become frustrated and mentally disengaged for the remainder of the session.

Task descriptions

As mentioned previously, studies are an artificial construct. Providing some context can make the tasks more realistic. However, task descriptions are best kept simple, so that the details don't confuse the participant. Consider the following task, for a participant that is asked to search for a winter coat on a retail site:

> *"Imagine that winter is coming. You have a brown winter coat that you bought two years ago when you went shopping with your sister who flew in from out of town for a few days. But you're not sure that the color of that coat will match the new pants you plan to buy. You think you'd like a blue coat. Using the site, search for blue coats."*

There is too much irrelevant information in this description. The extraneous details can distract the participant from the actual task. In addition, there is a reference to a sister. Not every participant will have siblings. We recommend sticking with more generic references; for instance, a friend.

Here is an improved, leaner version:

> *"Imagine winter is coming and you need a new coat. You'd like to buy a blue coat. Using the site, search for blue coats."*

This description provides enough context, without being overly specific.

Topics

Each task represents a number of topics to investigate. These topics depend on the goals of the study and the particular questions that the stakeholders have. The moderator uses probing questions to gain insights into these topics.

Let's use the example of a retail website again. Imagine that the stakeholders want to understand the following:

- Do users use autocomplete?
- Do search results seem relevant?
- Is navigating to the price filter in the search results page clear (for instance, this filter could be located below the fold on many smaller screens)?

The task description might be as follows:

Imagine you are looking for sneakers for yourself. Use the search bar and only look for sneakers that are within your price range.

Topics to investigate based on this task could include:

- Ease of locating the search bar
- Did the participant use the autocomplete? Why or why not?
- Relevance of the search autocomplete (for those that used it)
- Participant's impression of the relevance of the search results
- Ease of locating the price filtering option

A primary means of gaining insight into these topics is to observe the participant. The moderator can observe the participant to get information about the first two topics, since he can see whether it was easy for the participant to locate the search bar, and whether they used autocomplete.

A secondary means is the use of probing questions. If the autocomplete showed relevant terms and the participant did not use autocomplete, a probing question might be: "Let's talk for a moment about your use of the search bar. As you were typing, did you notice the options that showed up below where you were typing?" If the participant answers "yes", the moderator can follow up with another question; for instance: "You didn't use any of the autocomplete options that we presented to you. Can you tell me more about why that is?" By answering the probing questions, the participant supplies feedback on topics that were not initially covered.

Questions

Throughout the session, different types of probing questions are asked, depending on the purpose of the question.

The following are purposes for different types of probing questions:

- Feedback
- Elaborating
- Addressing missed topics
- Confirmation

Feedback

Feedback questions are generic questions to get feedback and determine the user's understanding and expectations.

Examples of feedback questions include the following:

- "Tell me what you see on this page."
- "What do you think you can do on this page?"
- "Let's say that you want to (buy this item). From here, what you do you think you would do?"
- "What would you expect if you tapped (this button)?"

Post-task questions are also feedback questions. Some common post-task questions are as follows:

- "In what you've just done, was there anything confusing?"
- "Was there anything that you would have liked to be different?"
- "Any other comments before we move on to the next task?"

Elaborating

Elaborating questions allow the moderator to get additional information on something the participant said or did. At times, it is possible to ask a question right after the event occurs, but other times, the question may have to wait. In that case, the reference to the action or quote must be added. Examples are as follows:

- Directly after the participant says something that requires elaboration: "Tell me more about that, or, How so?"
- "What were your thoughts when you clicked this?"
- "Tell me why you tapped (that button) first."
- "Earlier, you mentioned that (you didn't expect to see this here). Why do you feel that way?"
- "You said (you like this better). Can you talk a bit more about that?"
- "Is there anything specific about (this) that you like?"

Missed topics

These questions are used when a participant volunteered information about certain items or areas on a page, but didn't cover other areas that feedback was required for:

- "I know you mentioned (the title and the date). What about (the pictures)?"
- "You clicked on (this link and that link). What about [the other link]?"

Confirmation

This may be necessary if the participant volunteered information about a topic that requires quantitative information. For instance, if the stakeholders want to understand whether participants prefer scrolling or links to additional shorter pages, the goal is to report that a certain number of participants preferred one versus the other. The data should be self-reported, and thus, it needs to be explicitly asked, as follows:

- Participant: "It would be better if (there were more links)"
- Moderator: "Why?"

Post-session questions

These are questions that relate to the participant's overall experience while using the product. They can be feedback questions (as in the previous section) or benchmark score questions (see Chapter 2, *What Not to Forget When Planning Your Study*, for a list and information on the possible rating scales for the answers).

Examples of feedback questions are as follows:

- "How likely would you be to use this product in the future?"
- "How likely would you be to recommend this product?"
- "How easy to use/satisfying/useful/reliable do you feel this product is?"
- "What did you like about this product?"
- "What did you not like about this product?"
- "What was missing?"
- "How would you describe this product to others?"

Wrap-up

When the session is complete, the moderator thanks the participant. If compensation is provided, this is a good time to reiterate how the participant will receive their compensation.

Writing tips

The previous section provided examples of tasks and questions. In addition, there are some things worth mentioning about the overall discussion guide, addressed in the following sections.

Tone

The moderator's goal is to put the participant at ease and to get insights from participants. The tone that the moderator uses is an important factor in building this relationship. Imagine a study for an internal financial application used by fund managers. If we can describe fund managers in a general way, they are fast-paced adults with a head for numbers. Now, think about a study for an app that helps high school students explore career choices. Clearly, bonding with a high school student participant will require a less formal approach, as compared to the fund manager, and tasks should be set in the appropriate context.

Style

While tone is participant-facing, style refers to the way in which the moderator writes the discussion guide for their own use during the sessions.

There are two styles: a verbatim script, and a more concise list of bullet points.

There is no right or wrong approach to a discussion guide, as long as it helps the moderator to stay on track and cover what needs to be covered. Some moderators prefer a verbatim script, because it ensures that each participant receives an identical treatment. This, in turn, helps to avoid distortion in the results. Some prefer a verbatim script so that they can fall back on it. Others may feel more comfortable with bullet points, since they may find it easier to scan.

Examples of both discussion guide styles are available in the appendix.

Preparing for the study

In the previous chapters, we discussed finding participants and how many participants to invite to the study. The next step is to schedule the sessions. Before doing so, the study planning needs to be reviewed, because scheduling participants requires a lot of effort, and rescheduling participants not only requires additional effort but often results in losing participants.

Number of participants

We like to use around 10 participants per study, although we often go as low as 5 or as high as 15 participants. Since the sessions are moderated, the additional effort per participant is significant and must be taken into account in terms of the cost and schedule.

Days for the sessions

Based on the project schedule, it is important to finalize the dates for the sessions. We've had stakeholders who wanted to change the session dates, for instance, because they wanted to wait for the next release, in the case of a product under development. Changing the session dates requires rescheduling with the internal team, and most importantly, the participants.

Product being tested

The product being tested must be available before the moderator crafts the discussion guide; the moderator can not efficiently write tasks and questions without access to the product under testing.

Internal team

All team members that are helping out with the sessions must be identified, and their availability must be known before reaching out to participants. This includes the moderator, the technician that will help the participants with their setup, the schedule owner, and any observers.

Number of sessions per day

The number of sessions scheduled in a day depends on the duration of the session, how tight the project schedule is, and what must be done between sessions. Five to six one-hour sessions makes for a pretty full day.

Enough time has to be available between sessions to accommodate for sessions that are running over slightly. Time to reset or reload software or hardware between sessions, if necessary, must be taken into account, as well.

Bio breaks and lunch are necessities of life, and must be built into the schedule as well. Make sure that lunch is available for all team members. Appoint one team member to be in charge of lunch. A hungry moderator is not a happy moderator!

Time of day

Another consideration is during which parts of the day the participants are available. Depending on the type of product and the required participant profile, it is possible that the participants are busy at work during the daytime. In that case, a couple of sessions can be conducted early in the morning, before participants start their workday; perhaps a few can be run during the workday, and the bulk during the evening hours.

Dry run

The goal of a dry run is to test that the product can be accessed, that the remote moderated software setup works, and to try out the flow of the discussion guide. If the study sponsor wants to observe the dry run, they may expect to tweak the discussion guide based their observations. In this case, it is a good idea to have a preliminary dry run to test the mechanics before the second dry run with the study sponsor.

Results from the dry run may count as a valid session, as long as the session ran smoothly and the discussion guide was not significantly changed after the dry run.

Enough time should be available between the dry run and the first session to make any changes that are needed. A dry run might occur in the morning and the sessions might start in the afternoon of the same day. If a preliminary and second dry run are needed and the schedule permits, the preliminary dry run can be run in the morning, the second one in the afternoon, and the sessions can start on day two.

Backup slots

It is a good idea, if possible, to leave some time slots available for extra sessions at the end of the last day, for any last-minute additions. There are a variety of situations that may call for additional participants, including excessive no-shows, severe technical difficulties, a picky study sponsor who disqualifies participants based on the sessions, or a combination of all the above.

Floaters

The use of floaters is an alternative to backup slots. Floaters are backup participants that are on standby. We suggest assigning a floater to a group of sessions, such as the morning sessions, afternoon sessions, or evening sessions. Floaters are a quick fix and minimize the negative impact of a no-show, especially when observers are attending the sessions.

Sample schedule

A sample schedule for a study with 10 participants, when the majority of the participants work during the daytime, is as follows:

	Day 1	Day 2	Day 3
7:00 – 8:15			Participant 9
8:45 – 10:00	Dry run		Participant 10
10:30 – 11:45			
Lunch			
12:45 – 14:00		Participant 4	
14:30 – 15:45		Participant 5	
16:15 – 17:30	Participant 1	Participant 6	<extra participant if needed>
Dinner			
19:00 – 20:15	Participant 2	Participant 7	<extra participant if needed>
20:45 – 22:00	Participant 3	Participant 8	<extra participant if needed>

Communicating

Communication is always a crucial part of the success of any project that requires collaboration. Part of the UX researcher's responsibility is to communicate and build a relationship with the observers, as well as with the participants. Each requires a different approach.

Communicating with observers

Observers are often eager to see the final session schedule, so that they can plan their observation times. If the study participants represent multiple personas or use different devices (such as desktop versus mobile), observers will expect to see that information in the session schedule, so that they can choose to attend specific sessions based on their interests.

When communicating the schedule, it is important to set the expectation that this schedule may change; if a floater is required to participate, that floater may not correspond to the exact target group that was originally scheduled. The best possible resolution is to alert the observers to any changes as soon as possible.

Communicating with participants

Once participants have signed up for slots, calendar invites and frequent reminders (without being annoying about it) can help to ensure that the participants show.

If the participant needs to install any software ahead of the session, detailed instructions can be sent ahead of time, as well as the contact info for a technician on your end.

Communication tools

Scheduling, finalizing, and communicating the schedule can be a cumbersome task. Some remote moderated study tools include a scheduling management tool that automates scheduling, schedule changes, reminders, and notifications. This can be a huge time saver.

Being prepared for changes

As we mentioned previously, proper planning is crucial to a smooth study execution. However, things can still go wrong. People can get sick; bad weather and traffic can impact even remote studies, as participants can't make it home in time for their session; technology that worked one moment can stop working the next; and so on.

Make sure that you have a clear communication channel with the internal team members, participants, study sponsors, and observers, to notify everyone of any changes.

Pre-session tech setup

Remote studies require some level of setup on the participant's side. At a minimum, the participant needs access to the product under testing, and must be able to remotely communicate with the moderator and share the screen on the device that they are using. The webcam may also be shared.

Consumers and the general population are a target user group for many websites and apps. Study participants for these profiles are often not very tech savvy. This may present a challenge when software setup is required. Even if the setup is easy, participants may be intimidated by the prospect and feel uncomfortable.

While it sometimes makes sense to send out setup instructions ahead of time, it is a good idea to have a dedicated technician connect with the study participant right before the session (for example, 15 or 30 minutes in advance), to check the participant's setup and make them feel at ease. The less frazzled the participant is by the time the session starts, the better.

A pre-session check should include the following:

- Verifying audio clarity
- Ensuring that screen sharing is working and the screen is clear and crisp for everyone
- Ensuring that the webcam is working and is angled the correct way
- Ensuring that the screen mirroring to the desktop is working, if a mobile device is being used

Running the study

For the most part, running the study means executing the sessions. However, part of running an efficient and effective study is redirecting when needed; this can mean aborting a session when necessary, or deciding not to run certain sessions if they are not going to add any value.

Running the sessions

The moderator runs the session, yet the entire support team must be on deck behind the scenes; the technician must be available, in case something technical goes wrong during the session; for instance, if the moderating software crashes or the internet connection becomes unstable. The schedule organizer must be in contact with the moderator and observers, to inform them of last-minute participant changes.

When to abort a session

We already covered examples of when a session cannot be run or completed (for example, due to technical difficulties). There will be other times when it may be better to abort the session, rather than complete it. These situations can occur in spite of taking great care in recruiting.

The participant is not getting it

During the recruiting process, participants were screened and re-screened; they fit the profile, their command of the language was satisfactory, and they were able to communicate effectively.

Yet, during the session, the participant just doesn't *get* it; they don't understand the study approach, their feedback is irrelevant, and any efforts from the moderator to bring the participant back on track are in vain. This does happen. In these cases, it becomes clear that the session is a waste of time long before the session time is up. The decision to abort the session is usually made with a consensus from the team and the observers.

How to communicate this to the participant depends on how far into the session the abortion occurs. The UX researcher must make sure that the participant feels valued for their contribution regardless; there is no good reason to make him feel bad. The participant should also get their full compensation, as they used due diligence.

Mismatches in participants

Despite all of the hard work during the recruiting phase, two things can happen, covered in the following sections.

Someone other than the recruited participant joins the session

The person attending the session is not the person that was recruited. For instance, the husband shows up instead of the wife, or the daughter instead of the mother. There is a lack of understanding on the participant's side of how important the participant's profile is to the study.

Participant misrepresented themselves

The participant misrepresented themselves in the screener and re-screener. It is possible that the participant managed to misrepresent themselves without being detected, and the discrepancies only come to light during the study. For instance, the profile requires that the participant be the household member that makes decisions about car insurance. The screener may have included some proof of insurance, or other validating questions that the participant managed to answer. However, when asked specific questions about the insurance during the session, the participant cannot provide insightful feedback or relate past experiences.

Debriefing

An informal debriefing at the end of each day or after the sessions are all complete provides the study sponsors with a high-level overview while they are waiting for an in-depth report. If the debriefing occurs before all of the sessions are complete, it is possible that the sponsor wants to tweak the tasks and questions to focus more (or less) on certain areas or pain points. While this can yield additional valuable data, it can impact formal reporting. For example, if a task is added or removed midway, the reporting for that task will be based on fewer participants. This method may be more suitable when working in-house, or when the report is less important as a deliverable.

When enough is enough

As we described in `Chapter 2`, *What Not to Forget When Planning Your Study*, the number of study participants is defined as a part of the study preparation. There may be cases where it makes sense to wrap the study up before the full number of participants has completed the sessions.

Blocking usability issues

It is possible that a usability issue is related to the main features of that product. Thus, every participant using the product will encounter it and be blocked by it. Subsequent sessions will yield limited feedback due to this type of blocking issue. The decision can be made to halt the sessions and run another study only after those issues are fixed.

Blocking issues like this should be discovered by the UX researcher when they write the discussion guide. If that is the case, the UX researcher will inform the study sponsor while creating the discussion guide. However, the goal of a study is to gather user data, rather than to rely on an expert's review. The study may need to be run until enough data has been gathered to substantiate the findings.

Consistent feedback

Imagine that by participant 6 of 10, the user feedback is very uniform. If there is a consensus within the team that extra data is not going to enrich the findings, and if there are no contractual obligations to deliver a certain number of participants, it may make sense to wrap up the sessions.

Moderator techniques

Moderator techniques are simple to describe, but becoming a great moderator takes some practice. The following sections provide tips on how to be a good moderator.

The rules of the game

The moderator's goal is to gather insightful feedback. The moderator must do so in an objective and non-intrusive manner, while at the same time establishing rapport with the participant and ensuring their physical and psychological well-being. Striking this balance requires some practice.

A typical conversation between humans involves a level of interaction and sharing. For instance, a conversation between two peers could be a balanced exchange of thoughts and suggestions. A conversation between a manager and their team member might be more one-sided, but nonetheless, it is an exchange of thoughts, to some extent. A moderated session is a mostly one-sided conversation; the participant provides all of the information, while the moderator must show their engagement (as is expected in a human conversation) without truly adding to or influencing the conversation.

The moderator can carefully control their side of the conversation by using the types of questions that we discussed earlier, and by using other phrases in neutral ways. Examples include: o*k*, *Alright*, *Gotcha*, and so on. Such words must be spoken without an injection of emotion. For instance, a word such as ok is neutral if said in a neutral way, but can carry a meaning based on intonation; one can draw it out in a hesitating manner, which reflects, *Hmm, I'm not so sure about that*. Or, one can enthusiastically say, *ok!* Depending on the context, this could be interpreted as a confirmation or a relief (for example, it may be interpreted as a relief that the task is complete).

It is important to refrain from praising the participant (for example, saying *Good job!*), as they will see this is a positive reinforcement and validation. They may continue to look for validation as the session continues. Similarly, refrain from showing disapproval, as that may lower their confidence, making them think they did something wrong. Be neutral and friendly.

Participants may try to get confirmation through conversation, for instance, they may be asking for clarification of tasks or questions. When a participant is truly struggling with the completion of the task, it may be acceptable for the moderator to intercede and explain the task or question. Know that often, however, the participant is trying to get confirmation that they are doing well.

Dealing with participants that get stuck on a task or that are going down the wrong path may be tricky. If the task is a standalone task, meaning that no other tasks are building on it, the task can be abandoned without issue. However, if the task needs to be executed in order to provide the starting point for the next task, it is important to gently guide the participant (after that task has been recorded as a fail). If the participant realizes that they weren't able to complete the task and feels bad, it is important to iterate that we are not judging them and that this feedback will help make the experience easier for future users.

Once the session's tone is set, it will carry on throughout the session. That is why it is important to set the right tone from the start.

Understanding your participants

Participants can be categorized by their levels of engagement during the session, and by their dispositions, as covered in the following sections.

Level of engagement

The two extreme levels of engagement are the talker and the quiet type. Many participants fall somewhere in between.

The talker

The talker, as the term indicates, talks a lot. They easily go off on a tangent, and it may be difficult to interrupt them so that they can be redirected.

The quiet type

The quiet type doesn't say much, and won't elaborate on their own. This makes it hard to get enough insightful feedback. They are sometimes reluctant to say much, for fear of making a mistake. It may be helpful to remind the participant that we are not judging them, and that we are open to any feedback they may have.

Participant disposition

There are three common dispositions: the overly positive participant, the complainer, and the fixer. Many participants show a mixture of dispositions.

The pleaser

It is common human behavior to want to please, and this is especially reflected in artificial settings, such as studies. The overly positive person exhibits this tendency in a more extreme manner than most. They report liking pretty much everything that they encounter, or downplay any confusion or negative experiences. Their information is not very useful or insightful.

To redirect a pleaser, it can be helpful to refer to a setting outside of the study by asking: "If you were to use this product outside of this study, ...?" If the participant has given some examples of prior use earlier in the session, the moderator can refer back to those examples to frame the real-life reference, in an attempt get more realistic input.

The complainer

The complainer is someone that has a negative view of the product, the type of product, or life in general. They find fault with many things, and are prone to going off on a tangent.

It is important, yet sometimes challenging, to keep a balance between listening to the participant and indulging them. Generic words, as mentioned previously (such as ok), provide an acknowledgment that the participant was heard, without providing any elaboration or injecting bias.

Redirecting may build on the participant's sharing by asking them to imagine a more positive baseline experience to start answering from. For instance: "You mentioned that you would like to see (that functionality) in the product. If that was the case, what do you think about (this)?"

The fixer

The fixer not only notes an issue, but is quick to elaborate on a solution. While some thoughts on how to improve an experience may be helpful, the goal of a study is to gather user feedback, not in-depth, user-driven analysis.

Redirecting a fixer to focus on their experience may require considerable effort. On occasion, we've found that being straightforward about the desire to gather feedback rather than solutions works best.

Managing observers

Stakeholders are often eager to observe the sessions in real time, to get direct and immediate feedback.

The UX researcher must set clear expectations with the stakeholders ahead of the session. Occasionally, stakeholders expect to jump in mid-session and directly address the participant with additional questions. We don't allow stakeholders to do so, as it would negatively impact the continuity of the session and distract the participant. To make sure that observers don't give in to this temptation, the tool that is used for the sessions must be able to mute the observers. A web conferencing tool, for instance, allows the meeting organizer to mute certain parties.

Observers can share follow-up question requests during the session. This is usually done through a separate communication channel. Depending on the complexity of the product under testing, the disposition of the participant, the nature of the questions, and the moderator's ability to multitask, the moderator can choose to either address the questions during the session or wait until after the session.

It is also important to set realistic expectations on the scope and number of follow-up questions. Follow-up questions need to be limited; diving into an area of the product that is not currently in the scope is not an acceptable follow-up question.

Moderator note-taking

The moderator's primary job during a session is to observe and interact with the participant.

Generally, we prefer not to take obvious notes during sessions, except when the moderating software allows for real-time tagging. This is a very handy feature that makes it easy to take short notes that can be a huge time-saver during the analysis.

Instead, we recommend scheduling the sessions in such a way that there is a lot of time between them, so that you can document your observations while they are still fresh, before the next session begins. If this is not possible, then the second best option is to have a team member take notes.

Basic tool functionality

As promised earlier, this book is tool-agnostic. Any tool used must cover certain basic functionality, including the following:

- Viewing the participant's screen, hearing their audio, and optionally, viewing the webcam.
- Recording the session.
- Allowing observers and the option to mute observers.

Next steps

Once the sessions are complete, the recordings must be managed so that they are available for the UX researcher and stakeholders. This includes converting to a generic format (such as mp4), if necessary, providing clear and consistent filenames, and storing the data on a location that is accessible by all parties. If transcription services are used, the data must be delivered for transcription.

Any follow-up with the participants, including compensation, must also be dealt with.

The next step for the UX researcher is to analyze the data and write up the findings, as agreed upon during the study planning phase. The deliverables may include a topline report that is provided soon after the final session, so that stakeholders have a high-level overview while they wait for a more formal report. Analysis and report writing will be covered later in this book.

Summary

Running a remote moderated study allows for follow-up questions and stakeholder engagement through observations during the sessions, but it is a relatively time- and effort-intensive method.

If a quick turnaround time is paramount, and/or there are not enough resources to put in time and effort, a remote unmoderated study may be the better solution. We will discuss remote unmoderated studies with user videos in the next chapter.

5
Running a Remote Unmoderated Study with User Videos

As we mentioned in Chapter 1, *Why Everyone Should Run Remote Usability Studies*, in a remote unmoderated usability study, the UX researcher sets up the UX study and analyzes the results, but the participants complete the session when it is convenient for them, and without a moderator present. This allows the study participants to complete the study where and when it is most natural to them. In a video-based study, the participants deliver a user video detailing their experiences.

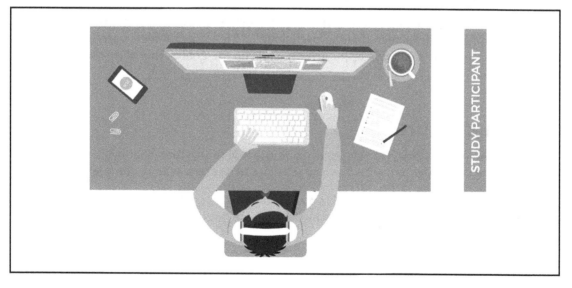

Video-based remote unmoderated study

This method is lightweight, has a quick turnaround time, and makes it easy to include participants from different locations who complete tasks in their own environments. User videos provide a firsthand account of how the user approaches a task, and of their feedback.

The challenges with this method include the inability to ask follow-up questions based on what is observed during the session and the inability to redirect participants in order to gain more insightful user feedback.

Major UX research tasks in video-based unmoderated studies include the following:

- Planning the study
- Recruiting and managing the participants
- Writing the script
- Preparing the participants for user videos
- Analyzing the data and writing the report

This chapter explains what user videos are, how to write a great script, and how to prepare the study participants for their user video sessions.

About user videos

A user video shows what the user experiences as they complete their task. At a minimum, it includes a capture of the screen that the participant is viewing and their narration. Whether a video-based study is a suitable approach depends on the goal of the study and the product under testing.

Screen capture

Screen capture options may vary depending on the tool or platform that is used. At a minimum, the user video must display the participant's screen as they complete the task.

Visual indications of mouse tracking (on a computer) or finger taps (on a touchscreen device) in the video are valuable additions to the recording, as it is otherwise difficult to follow what the user is doing.

Some user video tools additionally have the option to record the participant's facial expressions using a webcam on the computer or a mobile phone camera.

Audio capture

At the most basic level, the participant's audio must be captured, and should be clear and understandable. This means that the following criteria must be met:

- The volume must be loud enough
- The audio cannot break up significantly
- There must be consistency in volume and tone to avoid imbalanced audio
- There should be no background noise that impedes the audio quality, such as a hum from computer equipment, an air conditioning unit in the room, static noise, a child crying, or other disruptive household noises
- The participant must enunciate clearly
- If they are not a native speaker of the language of the study, their accent must be easy to understand

Think-aloud protocol

In a video-based, remote, unmoderated study, participants are asked to complete one or more tasks while using the think-aloud protocol.

The phrase *thinking aloud* refers to the participants speaking out loud what they are thinking as they complete each task. It is used in in-person and remote moderated studies. As mentioned in Chapter 4, *Running a Remote Moderated Study*, it is seen as a reliable method to gain insights into the participant's thoughts as they complete tasks.

The think-aloud protocol works well for unmoderated studies with user videos, but there are a couple of things to consider.

Formulating thoughts

Formulating thoughts is often a process rather than an instantaneous action; it can take a bit of time before the participant has completely formulated their thoughts. This manifests itself through incomplete sentences and switching between different topics. Participants may eventually summarize their completed thoughts, but it is often up to the UX researcher to interpret the thoughts and construct the final opinion.

Continued thinking aloud

Even when the instructions ask the participant to think aloud, it is common for study participants to forget to do so as they progress in the task or study. If the study consists of multiple tasks, it is a good idea to repeat the instruction to think aloud for every task.

Strengths of user videos

The main advantage of the video-based approach is that it enables the UX researcher to see exactly what the participant is doing when completing the task.

Observation of user actions

The UX researcher gets a firsthand review of every step and detail of the user's interaction with the product and interprets it accordingly.

Think-aloud verbal cues

Thinking aloud provides additional insight into how the participant feels about an experience. Pauses indicate that they may be searching for something or are not sure how to proceed, and sentiments such as frustration or delight can be heard in the participant's tone.

Facial expressions

If a webcam is used, observing facial expressions such as frowning or smiling can help round out the insights into user sentiment.

A picture is worth a thousand words

Showing the executive or development team a video clip of a user as they perform a certain action is more powerful than any description.

Suitable throughout the development cycle

The video-based approach is suitable for use in any product development stage that involves interaction with the product, such as interactive prototypes, early product releases, and live products. Static versions, such as wireframes, can also be tested, but as the strength of user videos lies in the observation of the interaction of the participant with the product under testing, this advantage is nullified if no interaction is possible.

Limitations of user videos

There are a few limitations of user videos that must be considered.

Privacy of user data

Banking and medical products, as well as electronic payment options, display personal information in tasks such as checking an account balance, making a transfer, viewing a medical history or paying a bill.

The participant must be given the opportunity to keep their information confidential. Some vendor platforms allow the participant to black out sensitive information before submitting their user videos. If this functionality is not available, the participant must be allowed to pause the recording while entering their private information. However, in some cases, this may make a user video useless if personal information is prevalent throughout the task. As an alternative, if the participant knows how to use a basic video editing tool, then they can manipulate the video before submitting. However, this option is not always feasible.

Another alternative is to provide test accounts for the product under testing. This may be somewhat less real life-like, but it removes the privacy issues. It can be a handy solution in cases where certain data must be prepopulated. Consider an investment banking app: the study participant may not have access to all the necessary information in their own account, such as investment buying or selling.

Digital rights management (DRM)

DRM is an approach to prevent unauthorized distribution of digital media, such as a recording of a movie. If the product under testing is a movie- or music-streaming app, then the user video cannot record the digital media in the app because of DRM restrictions. This can make the user videos mostly irrelevant; for instance, if the task is to add a caption or change subtitles to another language, then the user video will not be able to show that as the screen will be black during the recording.

Less deliberate feedback

Having the users say out loud what they are thinking as they complete each task while being recorded does not require the same kind of focus from the participants as responding in writing to a question in a survey. Having to write down a response requires more concentration, and some people will even reread and correct their responses in order to ensure that they correctly reflect their thoughts.

Because of this limitation, we often recommend using a hybrid survey and video approach in order to get the best of both worlds.

Session organization

The session must be organized based on the session duration, and the number of tasks and videos.

Session duration

A common rule of thumb for the duration of unmoderated user videos is up to 15 minutes. This is based on the popular belief that an individual's attention span is generally 10 to 15 minutes. This number has specifically been circulated in the context of learning, and has been adapted to gathering information in informal settings, such as a post-visit survey that site visitors can opt in to.

There is no strong scientific evidence to support this rule of thumb (as shown in a study by Karen Wilson and James Korn in 2007 (see `https://eric.ed.gov/?id=EJ772424 for more details`). Even if there was more solid scientific evidence, the level of complexity, variety in the task, personal engagement, and many other factors must be taken into account as well.

We routinely run studies with sessions of 30 to 45 minutes, and don't see any significant drop in attention or quality. Because the sessions are unmoderated, and we usually give the participants a few days to complete their session, we see that participants sometimes take breaks instead of completing the session in one sitting. As they are in their own environment, this could be because other aspects of their life interfere, or it may indicate that participants who get fatigued choose to take a break rather than continue and provide sub-optimal results. In any case, the participant should always be informed upfront as to how much of their time the participation in the UX study will require, allowing them to plan their schedule accordingly.

As we have mentioned in earlier chapters, there can be a large difference in the amount of time participants take to complete a task; some participants are quicker than others, and those who have issues completing the task will naturally take more time.

Number of participants

We typically use a similar number of participants as we would for a moderated study, around 8 to 12 participants.

Number of tasks

The number of tasks in a study can vary greatly depending on the predefined session duration and the length and complexity of the tasks.

Stakeholders may project the amount of time it should take a user to complete a set of tasks. However, they typically don't account for session setup and teardown time, nor the post-task or post-session survey questions. Their expectation of the time needed to complete a task may also be skewed because they might be basing it on the time it would take them, which is usually the time an expert user would take rather than a novice user, since the stakeholders work closely with the product. Time can also be different for someone who runs through the task in a test setting (merely clicking through) as opposed to someone who is completing the task in a real-life environment.

Number of videos

If the session consists of more than one task, there can either be a separate video file for each task or one video file containing all the tasks. A full-service vendor platform handles video management, and in that case, this is a moot point. In a do-it-yourself setup, however, it is a relevant issue.

There are advantages and disadvantages to each option. Multiple shorter videos are easier to manage in terms of video upload and file size and trying to find a specific part of the video (as the videos are shorter). Multiple videos, however, can create overhead since more videos need to be named correctly, uploaded, and so on. Regardless of the approach, the script must include instructions on how to deal with user videos.

The script

The UX researcher creates the script based on their conversations with the stakeholders about the main areas to be covered. The script is given to the study participants at the start of the study and includes the following:

- Introduction
- Instructions

- Tasks
- Optional post-task or post-session questions

A sample script is provided in the appendix of this book.

When using a vendor platform, the introduction and instructions are provided by the vendor and the UX researcher only needs to provide the tasks and any additional survey questions. When going the do-it-yourself route, the introduction and instructions are crucial to informing the participant and getting valid results.

Introduction

The study participants read these guidelines and instructions on their own before the study begins. Instructions should be clear and simple, and should include the following:

- A thank-you for participating.
- A description of what will happen in the session.
- An explanation that the goal is to get honest user feedback, and that there are no right or wrong answers. This should be an explicit invitation to provide feedback; some cultures are more reluctant to provide feedback, especially if it is negative.
- A listing of any limitations. If the product to be tested is a test version or a prototype, inform the participant of this and the possible consequences: There may be bugs, not all links will necessarily work, content may be missing or inconsistent, and so on.
- A confirmation of the expected schedule, including how much time the participant is allotted to complete the session and the expected amount of user effort.
- A contact email address and name, in case participants have questions.

Instructions

The instructions should include an explanation and examples of the think-aloud protocol, how to record videos, access to the product under testing, and the devices that are to be used for the study.

Think-aloud

As we mentioned previously, the main challenges with using the think-aloud method in an unmoderated setting are to make sure that the participant provides useful information and continues to talk out loud.

Give examples

In addition to describing what participants are asked to do, examples can be helpful. Provide an example of a poor and a good think-aloud session (in that order).

In a poor think-aloud session, the participant describes what they are doing rather than expressing their thoughts and opinions.

An example of a poor session might be: "I am now going to click the **Next** button. On this next page, I see the text box to enter my name. I will now enter my name." This is just a rundown of what a person is doing. It means that someone who can not see what is going on can still follow the actions, but that is beside the point.

In a good think-aloud session, the participant describes their feelings and expectations.

An example of a good session might be: "To continue, I will click the **Next** button. That is pretty clear to me." (Clicks and sees next page). "Hm, I had expected to see some more information and some options, but instead there is this form. It is a very long form. I am concerned that I am expected to provide a lot of personal information. I am not sure how I feel about doing that at this point in the process."

These examples can be provided in written format or in the form of a short video.

Greeting and task description

Ask the participant to start their user video by introducing themselves and the task. For example: "Hi, my name is Amy, and in this task, I will search for a pair of running shoes for myself." Introducing themselves as if they are talking to a person can help maintain a continuous think-aloud approach. By describing the task, the participant will focus on the task, and it will be apparent if the participant misunderstood the task. It's also handy for video reviewers, as it provides context.

Video recording

Some vendors provide a comprehensive platform for remote unmoderated video-based testing. These platforms provide an integrated environment for the UX researcher, as well as the study participant. The participants have been trained on how to use the platform.

With a do-it-yourself approach, the onus of identifying the tools and educating the participants on how to use those tools falls on the UX researcher. Standalone recording tools are available for many devices and operating systems. Even though they aim to be easy to install and use, this may be daunting to a target user who is not tech savvy. Common challenges include activating the touch indicator (that shows on screen where the user is tapping) in the mobile recording tool or ensuring that the webcam is pointed in the correct direction to record the facial expressions.

Instructions for audio and screen capture should include the following if applicable:

- Installing (if required) and starting the tool
- A dry run to verify the following
  - That the correct browser tab is recorded
  - That the audio is clear and the volume is right
  - That the touch indicator is activated
  - That the webcam is working and angled the correct way, and that the correct camera is recording when multiple cameras are on a single device

Strongly suggest to the participant that they do a test run before they start the actual study.

Video file format, size, and delivery

In a vendor platform, the video formatting and delivery are built-in functions. The participant does not need to concern themselves with this.

When using a standalone tool, the participants must be instructed as to which output format and resolution to use. Resolution is important as it influences the quality and size of the file. The goal is to provide user videos that have a high enough resolution to be clear and large enough, but that are as compact as possible. mp4 is a universal file format that is supported by many tools, and can be viewed by most operating systems without much extra effort.

The instructions must clearly indicate how the video files are to be delivered—for instance, using an online storage medium.

Access to the product under testing

The script must provide clear instructions that outline how to access the product under testing, such as a link to the app in the store or a URL to the prototype. Credentials need to be provided if required.

Device to be used

Participants are recruited based on a specific device. Confirm the device that they are expected to use.

Read task instructions

The participants should be instructed to read the task instructions completely before starting the recording. This will reduce interruptions of the recording in order to refer back to the instructions.

Tasks

In order to yield insightful user videos, a balance between task complexity, duration, and ease of completion is crucial. We describe this in more detail in the following section, and provide pointers to get the most out of user videos.

Tasks that are easy to complete

Tasks that are very simple and easy to complete may not yield much insight into the user's experience. For instance, if a call to action is clearly displayed on the homepage, and the task is to find that call to action, users will likely provide very little feedback. They will look at the homepage, perhaps scroll a bit, and then click or tap the call to action. The goal of including simple tasks in a study could be to confirm a predefined notion that a task is easy to complete; it should not be added with the expectation that it will yield large amounts of insights.

Tasks that are difficult to complete

Tasks that are difficult to complete can pose a real problem for unmoderated studies. Since there is no moderator to keep the participant on track, it is entirely possible that participants will go in the wrong direction and will not complete the task. This can be disheartening for the participant, and they may become less confident or more negatively disposed towards the product and the study. This, in turn, can negatively influence the rest of the session.

If a task is expected to be difficult for some participants, the script can help mitigate the negative feelings:

- When the task is introduced to the participant, restate that "we are not testing you".
- Provide the participant with a timeout time. This is the maximum time that a participant should spend on trying to complete the task.
- Stress that the goal is to complete the task, and that you want them to do their best, but that it is ok if they can't complete the task.

Complex tasks

The complexity of a task needs to be borne in mind. Changing the quantity of an item on a product details page, for instance, is a simple task; it only requires one click, and usually follows design best practices (a drop-down element). A complex task is a task that requires a lot of the user's concentration. It may involve selecting or entering a lot of information, be longer and cover multiple steps, or involve a complicated subject matter. As a result, participants may spend less time talking out loud about their impressions and feelings because they are occupied with the task itself. In such cases, it may be helpful to reiterate to the study participant that proper thinking aloud is crucial.

Long tasks

Sometimes tasks are very long. This may not pose a problem if the task is straightforward, such as using a wizard that requires simple information input only, or a commonly understood flow, such as choosing and purchasing an item in an online clothing retail store.

If, however, the task is long and possibly complex, it might be better to split the task up into smaller tasks, if possible. These smaller tasks need to be able to stand on their own so that the one task has a natural endpoint and the next task has a natural starting point. If these are not natural, the participant may get confused, which in turn may negatively impact their experience and the completion of the task.

There are no hard and fast rules to decide when to split up a task. In one application, the task of editing information, saving, and confirming that the edits have been made can be simple, and can all occur on the same screen. It would be detrimental to split it up into multiple tasks. In another application, however, the design could be less intuitive, and the actions could span multiple pages, which would make it a good candidate for splitting up.

Goal-oriented tasks

If the participant has a goal, they will use the product under testing based on that goal. It is therefore best to always give participants a goal-oriented task. Instead of asking participants to give their first impressions of a homepage (not a very goal-oriented task), ask them to complete a task and consider a hybrid method (see `chapter 7`, *Running a Remote Unmoderated Study with a Hybrid Approach*) to gather additional first impressions.

Post-task or post-session questions

It is not uncommon to add a couple of post-task or post-session questions. The think-aloud data in user videos provides a wealth of qualitative information, but sometimes it is useful to have some quantitative information as well—for instance, to compare the results of different versions of a product, or because some stakeholders or sponsors feel more comfortable with quantitative information. The quantitative information that is gathered from a small sample size is best treated as an indicator only.

Common post-task questions include the following:

- **Ability to complete the task**: "Were you able to complete the task?".
- **Ease of completing the task**: "How easy or difficult was it to complete the task?".
- **When a task was difficult to complete**: "Please explain your answer."

Common post-session questions start with "Based on your experience in this study", and include the following:

- "How many stars would you give this product?"
- "What did you like most about this product?"

- "What did you like least about this product?"
- "How likely would you be to use this product in the future?"

Chapter 6, *Running a Remote Unmoderated Study with a Survey*, focuses on survey-based remote unmoderated studies, and provides a closer look at survey question types.

Writing tips

In a remote unmoderated setting, the script is the main (and often only) way to provide information to the study participant. The script must be comprehensive, informative, and easy to understand, yet concise. Maintaining this balance can be challenging.

Provide a clear starting point for each task

The task description must clearly indicate how or where to start the task. Stakeholders often adopt an internal naming system to refer to pages within the product. These names are not always clear to outsiders who have no knowledge of the product. Instead of using these naming conventions, a task should include the title or the URL of the page—if applicable—or a screenshot of the page or screen to ensure that all participants understand where to start a task.

If a subsequent task is provided, it is important to make sure that all participants start the task at the correct location. This may be especially relevant if the previous task was difficult to complete, meaning that participants may not all be at the same point in the interface. Providing the URL or screenshot again will ensure that user feedback covers a common set of pages or actions.

Tone

The goal of the script is to provide all relevant information to the study participant in a clear, comprehensive, and concise manner. It is also one of the few ways to build rapport with the participants. The tone should be friendly and address the participant demographic, if relevant. For instance, a script aimed at children should use simple words and sentence structure, while a script aimed at non-technical users should avoid using technical terms.

Preparing for the study

Once the tasks have been created and the script has been crafted for a do-it-yourself approach, or the study has been set up in the vendor platform, there are just a few more things to check before starting the study:

- Check the product under testing to make sure that participants can access it. This includes checking the URL, credentials, or the installation of an executable.
- Perform a dry run of the tasks.
- Check that the script contains all necessary information or perform a dry run of the study in the vendor platform.
- If the study is a team effort, make sure that one person is appointed as the main point of contact. This person should be available to follow the progress of the sessions, and should be ready to jump in should participants have questions.
- Typically, user feedback will be delivered within a short timeframe. Now is a good time to determine who will review the results, and to clear that person's schedule for the appropriate times.

Scheduling participants

Once participants have been recruited as described in `Chapter 3`, *How to Effectively Recruit Participants*, it is much easier to schedule their participation than it is for remote moderated sessions. Participants only need access to the script and the product under testing, and they need to understand when the user videos must be completed by. As described previously, this is part of the script instructions.

Even though participants have been vetted for, been notified of, and confirmed their participation in the study, some participants will not complete the study, for one reason or another. In addition, some user videos may be of poor quality and lack insights because the audio or video elements are missing. We usually over-invite by 30% to cover these cases.

As an alternative, it is possible to invite the exact number of participants and only add more participants when it becomes clear how many participants are not completing the study. This approach will possibly reduce the total reward or compensation that will be paid out, but it can take a bit longer to get all the submissions.

Running the study

As mentioned previously, the study will run itself since the participants have all the necessary information to complete the session. The main point of contact should keep track of the progress.

As the submissions come in, the UX researcher can do a quick review to ensure that the participants completed the session as expected and provided meaningful comments.

If the insights are not as useful as expected, there may be an opportunity to go back to the study participant and ask them to elaborate. If a follow-up is possible and is desired, it is best to do this as soon as possible so that the study participants still have their experience fresh in their mind.

A rookie mistake is to ask study participants to redo their session. This might come up because there is an issue with the recording, for instance. It is typically not a good idea to have a participant run through the same tasks twice; any first impressions will be compromised, and participants will have different and less feedback about the tasks. The desired approach is to remove any results that are not valid and add additional participants to the study instead.

Next steps

Once the recordings are completed, they must be available to the UX researcher and any other team members for review and analysis. This either includes ensuring that the right set of people has access to the vendor platform or putting the mp4 files in a shared location for easy access.

Analyzing user videos is a time-consuming task; we estimate that proper analysis and documentation of the issues can take up to 3 or 4 times the duration of the user videos. For instance, if 10 participants provided a total of 80 minutes' worth of videos, the analysis time will take approximately 240 minutes, or 4 hours. We will cover analysis in `Chapter 8`, *What to Consider When Analyzing and Presenting the Study Results.*

Summary

Remote unmoderated user videos are a great way to gather some quick user feedback and to view how participants interact with a product. The think-aloud protocol in particular is a very useful methodology. Video-based studies can be run using a vendor platform or a do-it-yourself approach. While the latter requires more effort, both are viable options, depending on budget and resources.

An alternative to video-based studies are survey-based studies. Chapter 6, *Running a Remote Unmoderated Study with a Survey*, describes the details of survey-based remote unmoderated studies.

6
Running a Remote Unmoderated Study with a Survey

As we mentioned in `Chapter 1`, *Why Everyone Should Run Remote Usability Studies*, in a remote unmoderated usability study, the UX researcher sets up the UX study and analyzes the results, but unlike a moderated study, the participants complete the session without a moderator present. The study participants complete the study tasks where and when it is most natural to them.

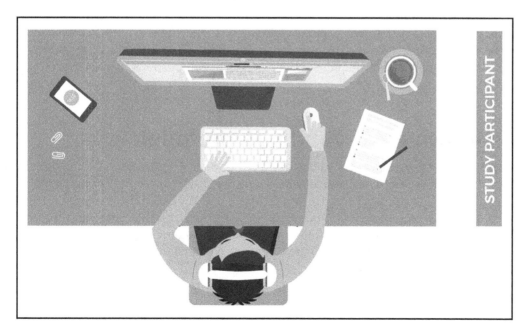

Survey-based remote unmoderated study

In a survey-based unmoderated study, the deliverable consists of answers to a set of questions based on tasks that the user completed. This method is lightweight, has a quick turnaround time, and the participant feedback is easy to digest in its written format. Challenges with this method include the inability to ask follow-up questions or view the exact path the user completed, as there is no real-time observation or user video.

The major UX research efforts in unmoderated studies include the following:

- Planning the study
- Recruiting and managing participants
- Writing the script
- Analyzing the data and writing the report

This chapter explains what surveys are and how best to use them, how to write an efficient script, and how to prepare the participants for their unmoderated session.

About surveys

In survey-based remote unmoderated studies, tasks and questions are shared with participants in a survey format. Participants complete tasks on their own and in their own environment by reading task instructions and answering questions after completing the task. Once all tasks are completed, the participant answers post-session questions based on their overall experience with the product during the study. The questions can include closed questions, such as rating questions, as well as open questions to gather qualitative user feedback.

Write-down-what-you-think protocol

Moderated and user video-based studies use the think-aloud protocol to gain insight into the user's thoughts as they complete a task. The phrase "thinking aloud" refers to the participants speaking out loud what they are thinking as they complete each task. In a survey-based study, this principle is adapted to a "write-down-what-you-think" protocol. Similarly to the think-aloud approach, the participant is encouraged to think out loud and is then asked to write down what they are thinking. We have found that using this protocol yields a lot of insightful feedback.

Strengths of surveys

There are a number of advantages to using survey-based approaches, including a more detailed look at the user experience when completing longer-running tasks and the ability to dig deeper into certain areas of the application.

Long tasks

Some tasks, such as a multistep onboarding task or a digital checkout, cover a longer user journey. If the participant completes the entire task and only gets to answer questions after the entire task has been completed, they may not remember all the details, especially of their experience during the earlier part of the task.

Consider a checkout process, starting with adding an item to the cart and ending with a completed purchase. This multistep process can be broken down into subtasks, such as adding an item to the cart, updating the cart, and checking out. The checkout itself can include entering the billing, shipping and payment information, making the purchase, and reviewing the confirmation.

While on the cart page, the participant may, for example, notice that a **Continue Shopping** button is missing. It is unclear whether they will still remember this detail once they get to the post-task questions.

Dividing this task into subtasks and asking questions after each step yields more detailed feedback. If the participant viewed the cart page and was immediately asked for their feedback, the lack of a **Continue Shopping** button would be at the top of their mind, and would be far more likely to be reported.

Deep dive questions

Imagine a situation where analytics logs indicate that a significant number of users drop off at a certain point in the user journey. User videos of participants completing the journey may provide some indications as to the issue, but a user video provides no opportunity to ask questions about a specific point in the user journey.

A survey-based approach, similar to a moderated study, can gather feedback from the participant at that particular point by asking a number of probing questions to understand the participant's sentiment and gain additional feedback. The questions might center around the ease-of-use, the level of confidence in the successful completion of the task, how obvious the next step is, whether the participant would continue if they were using the product outside of the study, their impressions of the page or functionality, and so on. It is often helpful to ask a few similar questions to get at the problem from different angles and elicit additional feedback.

Suitable throughout the development cycle

The survey-based approach is suitable for use with any product under testing, including static wireframes, interactive prototypes, products under development, and live products. Instructions inform the user of any limitations of the product, and these instructions can be repeated throughout the survey if needed.

Very complex prototypes with predefined paths that constrain the participant to follow an exact sequence of clicks might pose a problem, however, because there is no way to guide the participant back on to the right path if they get lost. One way to mitigate this issue could be to offer a clickable table of contents for the prototype, and at the beginning of each task, ask the participant to navigate to the corresponding point in the prototype using the table of contents. If they cannot complete a task, they are then not hindered from completing subsequent tasks. Another possibility is to provide the path instructions of the previous task at the beginning of each new task. This ensures that if a participant did not previously navigate correctly, all participants start the next task at the correct position in the prototype.

Larger number of participants

The survey-based unmoderated method works well with sample sizes that are slightly larger than the ones typically used in the user video-based approach because written feedback is quicker to analyze than user videos, and participant sessions are easier to complete for study participants. We routinely use 15 to 25 participants in a survey-based study. The results provide quantitative indicators, as well as qualitative feedback.

Limitations of surveys

The survey-based approach has some limitations that need to be considered, as explained below.

Not ideal for path analysis

If the goal of the study is to understand the specific path that a user follows through the product, a user video is the preferred approach as it provides visual context. Survey participants can be asked to report the path that they took, but this information could be incomplete or inaccurate, and the UX researcher has no way to verify what is reported. If the goal is to document which of the multiple entry points the participants chose, such as whether they started a journey from the top menu or the homepage, then this could be done in a survey. Anything more extensive is not recommended.

Fraud

It is possible that survey participants don't fully engage in completing the tasks and only provide the bare minimum of feedback. It is also possible for a participant to take the survey multiple times. This defeats the purpose, as first impressions and a fresh approach to the tasks and questions are necessary to yield reliable results. Even when a repeat participant tries to mimic their first go through a survey, they tend to rate more favorably, provide less feedback, and be more forgiving of any issues.

The variety of devices that can be included in a remote study is a major advantage of unmoderated studies, yet, especially in a survey-based study, there is no way of confirming this information, and it is, therefore, possible that participants use a device other than the one they were recruited to test. This may be on purpose (perhaps they do not have easy access to the intended device at the time of the session) or it may be an honest mistake.

A few tips for spotting fraudulent entries:

- If available, validate that the system-recorded IP addresses match the location of the participants.
- Check for duplicates in the system-recorded IP addresses, if available.
- Check the system-recorded duration of the session. In an unmoderated study, participants can take as many breaks as they want, so the time in session is not an accurate measurement of the length of a session. It is, however, a great way to spot cheaters. If a session was designed to take 45 minutes to complete, and an entry was completed in 10 minutes, it is fair to discard this submission.
- An entry that has mostly (or only) the most positive rating—or a certain pattern of rating selections—and has short answers (some text analysis and survey tools will let you check for that) that don't carry any meaning is a likely sign of someone who did not really apply themselves to the tasks.

- It is possible to add some rating questions with reverse-order scales to check how well people are paying attention. However, the danger here is that people may pay attention to the task, but not the labels for the answers, especially in a matrix question. Their response will show as a false negative, not because they are not diligent in completing the tasks, but because they have gotten used to the order of the answer choices.

Self-reported data

While self-reported data is a valuable source of user feedback, the survey-based approach relies solely on self-reported data. Participants may contradict themselves without realizing, or what they report could differ from what they actually did, perhaps because they feel self-conscious about their performance. There is a large body of literature available that talks about how what we do and what we say we do are not always the same.

Qualitative feedback from non-native speakers, from people who are not great communicators, and from those who are more reserved can be disappointing as it often does not contain a lot of information. Providing upfront instructions asking the participants to elaborate and use clear and full sentences can help alleviate this issue to some extent. The downside of such instructions is that participants may feel forced into providing details, even if they really don't have anything to contribute, and they may fabricate things to make sure they are viewed as doing a good job and can claim their reward for participating.

Because of the limitation with self-reported data, we often recommend also collecting user videos as a secondary source to investigate areas of concern.

Survey questions

Every one of us has participated in a survey at one time or another. Some surveys are easy to understand and others not so much. Much of the power of good surveys lies in writing good questions and providing optimal answer choices. There is a lot that goes into writing good surveys and describing every aspect of it is beyond the scope of this book.

Selecting the appropriate question type plays a crucial role in writing good questions. Most survey tools feature a substantial list of question types. All question types have their own use, but at the end of the day, there are a few question types that can perform the majority of the work. This section describes those main question types and their use.

Based on the type of information that questions yield, there are open and closed questions.

Open questions

Open questions have one or more textboxes for the participant to provide their feedback. They are used to gather qualitative feedback.

Qualitative feedback questions include standalone questions that can be used when eliciting thoughts and feedback with as little guidance as possible. The following are some examples of such questions:

- Initial impressions:
    - "Please have a look at the homepage, but don't click on anything yet. Write down your impressions:"
    - "Write down any comments you have about this page:"
- Post-session questions:
    - "What did you like most?"
    - "What did you like least?"
    - "What functionality would you like to see added?"
    - "What would make you more likely to use the product in the future/recommend it to others?"

Open-ended questions can be displayed as single-line, multiline, or multiple separate entry areas:

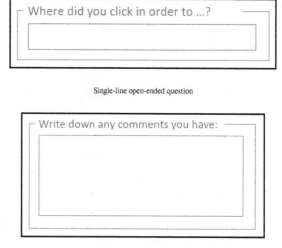

Single-line open-ended question

Multiline open-ended question

What did you like most?

1:

2:

3:

Multi-entry open-ended question

Open-ended questions are frequently used as an elaboration to a rating question. For instance, a rating question about the ease-of-use of a task is often followed by "Please explain your answer:".

The drawback of open-ended questions is that it can be time-intensive to analyze this data, and it might not always be possible to determine a clear sentiment in the response. An alternative is to use a hybrid form of open and closed questions. For instance, instead of an open-ended question about first impressions, it is possible to direct the answer in a positive or negative direction by offering the choices "mostly positive, because…" or "mostly negative, because…".

Closed questions

Closed questions are questions that present the participant with a predefined set of answers to choose from. They are commonly referred to as multiple-choice questions. The same rule about leading questions also applies to the responses. The responses should allow the participant to choose the response that they find most appropriate. This requires that the UX researcher carefully scrutinizes the provided options in order to avoid the following eventualities:

- A **"This does not apply to me" option is missing**: For example, the responses "Yes" and "No" for the question "Did you notice that …?" cover all possibilities, whereas for the question "Do you travel mostly for business?", it would be prudent to add an "I don't travel" option instead of forcing the participants to choose an option that does not apply to them. Similarly, when asking a participant to rate how easy or difficult a task was to complete, for example, an "I could not complete the task" option should always be offered for the same reasons.

- **Not all possible responses are offered**: For example, the question "At which banks are you currently a customer?" could offer a list of obvious candidates, but should also offer an "Other (please specify):" option, allowing participants to add a different answer.
- **There are gaps**: The responses to a question like "How often do you….?" should not only offer "Daily", "Monthly", and "Yearly" as response choices. Participants would not be able to respond with once or twice a week, for example.

Single-answer multiple-choice questions

These questions allow for only one answer and use radio buttons. An example is a question about the participants' age range:

```
┌─ Please select your age group: ──────────────┐
│                                               │
│   ◯  Under 24 years old                       │
│                                               │
│   ◯  25 -34 years old                         │
│                                               │
│   ◯  35 – 44 years old                        │
│                                               │
│   ◯  45 – 54 years old                        │
│                                               │
│   ◯  Over 54 years old                        │
│                                               │
└───────────────────────────────────────────────┘
```

Single-answer multiple-choice question

The responses in multiple-choice questions should always be mutually exclusive.

UX study surveys frequently use multiple-choice questions for ratings. A popular rating scale is the Likert scale. Likert scale questions come in all shapes and sizes. As we mentioned in `Chapter 2`, *What Not to Forget When Planning Your Study*, we prefer using 5-point scale, labeled rating questions ordered from the most negative to the most positive, with a neutral element in the middle.

This is quite the mouthful, but you can see the details of this arrangement in the following image:

5-point scale labeled question ordered from the most negative to the most positive, with a neutral element

Let's examine the individual elements of this arrangement:

- **Five-point scale**:
  - Best practices dictate that a scale should not extend to less than 3 or more than 11 points. Most UX researchers prefer a 5-point or 7-point scale. We prefer a 5-point scale because it provides the participant with enough options without overwhelming them and possibly making it difficult for them to choose the "correct" rating.

- **Labeled scale points**:
  - The phrase "labeled" refers to having text on scale points rather than numbers. Labels provide guidance and can be added to each scale point or only to the endpoints. We prefer labeling each scale point in order to remove any ambiguity.
  - When using labels, the labels should always be balanced—that is, the same weight should be used on either end of the scale and the same number of negative and positive elements should be used each time.

- **Most negative to most positive**:
  - Many UX researchers order the scale points from most positive to most negative. We have found that the inverse can help reduce the tendency of participants to veer towards more positive ratings. The participants are often anchored by the first choice presented to them and then reevaluate this first choice with each subsequent option until they encounter one they find more fitting.

- **Odd number of scale points**:
  - An odd number of scale points allows for a neutral option (one that is neither positive nor negative). Proponents of the odd-number scale argue that a neutral option allows a participant who truly doesn't have an opinion to express that opinion properly, since a 4-point scale will force a participant to choose either a negative or a positive option. Proponents of the even-number scale argue that participants may take the easy way out by selecting a neutral option, thus leaving the UX researcher with very little informative data. We very much prefer the odd-number scale and have not experienced a pronounced tendency towards the neutral option.
- **Single question or question matrix**:
  - Single-answer, multiple-choice questions can be presented as a single question or a matrix of questions.
  - Matrix questions are a bit controversial. On the one hand, they are an efficient way of gathering information about many aspects of a user's experience in a condensed manner. On the other hand, some UX professionals object to the leading nature of the statements. To alleviate this, positive and negative statements can be alternated. We have unfortunately found that this might lead to inconsistent results, most likely because participants aren't reading the statements closely enough. Another alternative is to present each statement as a single question and craft each question carefully. This, in turn, removes the efficiency and may lead to survey fatigue.

The following image shows a survey question that incorporates all of these elements:

Please rate the following statements:	Strongly disagree	Somewhat disagree	Neither agree nor disagree	Somewhat agree	Strongly agree
The information seems complete	○	○	○	○	○
The reviews are easy to locate	○	○	○	○	○
The images are useful	○	○	○	○	○

Multiple-choice matrix question

Multi-answer, multiple-choice questions

Multi-answer, multiple-choice questions are also called checkbox questions. More than one option can be selected, as shown in the following image. They can be presented as a single question or a matrix:

Multi-answer, multiple-choice question

Semantic differential scale

A semantic differential scale is a closed question that will yield the participants' perception of the product under testing (or an aspect of it) based on their rating of pairs of bipolar adjectives that describe it, such as "active" and "passive", or even phrases such as "large product range" and "narrow product range".

By listing both bipolar adjectives, semantic differential scales help in formulating questions more neutrally than using a Likert scale would. With a Likert scale, a question could be "Please rate this statement: I found the website to be attractive.", while the semantic differential equivalent would be "I found the website to be …" and the participant would choose between the adjectives "attractive" and "unattractive".

It is also more efficient than using multiple Likert scales when the statement is essentially identical and only the adjectives vary, as shown in the following image:

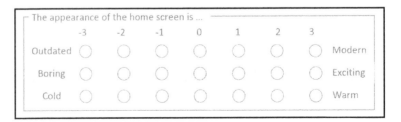

Semantic differential scale

Ranking questions

In a ranking question, the participant is given a number of options and asked to rank them, for example, by order of importance. For instance, if a company has a number of ideas for a new functionality that they wish to implement in the next release, and they want to understand what might be the most desired functionality, a ranking question can help, as shown in the following image:

Rank the following features according to their importance.
(drag and drop the feature to move to the appropriate rank)

1	Share with friends
2	Send email
3	Save to external source
4	Toggle light
5	Auto-save mode

Ranking question

Ranking questions are useful, but can easily become very confusing for the participant. They should only be used when there are only a few possible options to rank. It is important to inform the participant how to use the question. For example, if the survey tool allows the participant to drag and drop the option into its spot in the ranking order, then this should be explicitly stated in the question.

Ranking questions, however, do not provide an indication of how desirable an option is to the user and how the desirability of the options are related to each other. For instance, a participant may find three of the five options equally very important, while the other two are not important at all. It is not possible to express this with a ranking question. Grouping questions can help overcome this limitation.

Grouping questions

Grouping questions can be used for card-sorting analysis. There are two versions: open and closed card-sorting analysis. For a closed sort, the participants are given a set of predefined options and a number of predetermined buckets to sort these options into. Both the number of each and the labels are predefined. This is helpful when investigating the information hierarchy of a content-heavy website.

Another use may be, as mentioned previously, grouping functions according to their importance, as shown in the following image:

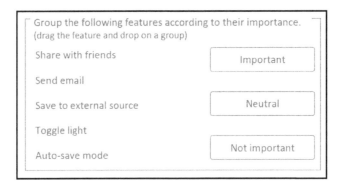

Grouping question

In an open card-sort analysis, respondents can choose their own categories and labels. They are then provided with a number of items to sort.

The most common survey tools include a number of question types and have extensive help documentation to explore.

Study organization

The study must be organized based on the session duration, the number of participants, and the tasks.

Session duration

Survey-based sessions are best kept to about 45 to 60 minutes. There is an inverse correlation between the length of surveys and the quality of the responses. If each time the participant selects "next" in a survey, they are confronted with an even longer page of open questions, how likely are they to keep providing a lot of good input? In any case, the participant should always be informed upfront as to how much of their time the participation in the UX study will require, allowing them to plan their schedule accordingly.

There can be a large difference in the amount of time participants take to complete a task; some participants are quicker than others, and those who have issues completing the task will naturally take more time. The session duration should therefore be estimated based on the average task completion duration.

Number of participants

We typically use 15 to 25 participants in a survey-based study. It is possible to use more participants compared to a video-based study, since the workload on both the participants and the UX researcher is lighter.

Number of tasks

The number of tasks in a study can vary greatly depending on the session duration and the length and complexity of the tasks.

Stakeholders may project the amount of time it should take a user to complete a set of tasks. However, they typically don't account for session setup and teardown time, nor for post-task or post-session survey questions. Their expectation of the time needed to complete a task may also be skewed, because they base it on their own time, which is usually the time an expert user would take rather than a novice user. Time can also be different for someone who runs through the task in a test setting (merely clicking through) versus someone who is completing the task in a real-life environment.

The script

The UX researcher creates the script based on their conversations with the stakeholders about the main areas to be covered. The script is provided to the study participants at the start of the study and should include the following:

- Introduction
- Instructions
- Tasks
- Optional post-task or post-session questions

A sample script is provided in the appendix.

Introduction

The introduction should include the following:

- A thank-you for participating.
- A description of what will happen in the session.
- An explanation that the goal is to get honest feedback and that there are no right or wrong answers. It should include an explicit invitation to provide feedback because some cultures are more reluctant to provide feedback, especially if it is negative.
- A listing of any limitations, such as whether the product under testing is a prototype or a test version. Inform the participant of this and the possible consequences: there may be bugs, not all links will necessarily work, and content may be missing, or may not be live content.
- A confirmation of the expected schedule, including how much time the participant has to complete the session and the expected amount of user effort.
- A contact email address and name in case participants have questions.

Instructions

The instructions explain how to properly execute the write-down-what-you-think protocol and cover guidelines that relate to logistics, such as the devices and software to be used.

Write-down-what-you-think protocol

The protocol is described and examples are provided to illustrate what a good and a bad session are like.

Access to the product under testing

A pointer to the product under testing can be a URL for a website, possibly with a set of credentials to access a site that is still under development. For an app, this is a link to the store or build-distributing apps, or even the build files themselves, if the app is still under development.

Device to be used

Participants were recruited based on a specific device. The device they are expected to use is confirmed in this section.

Tasks versus questions

Especially when testing prototypes, it is good practice to clearly differentiate between tasks that require the participant to do something with the product being tested and questions (post-task or post-session) that are meant to elicit feedback on the experience. One way of doing this is to consistently prefix tasks with a "Task:" label and questions with a "Question:" label in the survey and add an explanation of this convention to the instructions.

Tasks

There is a lot of flexibility in the length and complexity of tasks in a survey-based study.

Task context

For each task in the survey, the UX researcher should make sure that they provide the context for the task in the question description. For example, not everyone might be interested in buying a loudspeaker online, but if this is the only product that is orderable in the prototype under testing, then the task context could state "Imagine that you are looking for a portable loudspeaker, either for yourself or for someone in your family…". Similarly, if presenting screenshots in a survey-based study, it is advisable that you add some context along the lines of "Imagine that you just logged in to the banking app as Peter Smith and you are now viewing your account balance…". The aim is that the participant identifies with and owns the task, thinking "I am Peter Smith" instead of thinking "this is Peter Smith's account balance I am looking at".

Task flow

The order of the tasks may be dictated by necessity. If, for example, it is necessary to log in to or register with the product before being able to use it, then these tasks obviously have to be performed first.

Where this is not the case, the tasks should be ordered in such a manner that the previous questions do not reveal too much about what will be asked in subsequent questions. For example, if the participant is first asked to update their account information, and then a couple of tasks later, they are asked where they would expect to find language preference settings (which are in the same submenu as the account information), then they will probably have noticed the language preference settings when they were searching for the account information previously, and as such will all provide the correct response, wrongly suggesting that everyone found it immediately.

If there are no such restrictions, then it is a good idea to start with the longer, more complex tasks after an initial warm-up task or two, and end with easier ones when the participant's concentration might be waning.

Branching can be used in the survey to present the most appropriate questions and answer options to the participant. For example, a question that refers to a feature that is only available on devices of the latest generation can be configured in the survey tool to only be shown when the current participant selected one of the eligible devices as the one that they are using. This results in the task flow being different for different participants.

Tasks that are easy to complete

A survey is a great way to confirm whether tasks that are thought to be easy to complete are, in fact, easy for prospective users. A single question about the ease-of-use with optional elaboration by those who found it difficult to complete doesn't take a lot of effort from the participants to respond to, or for the UX researcher to analyze.

Tasks that are difficult to complete

If a task is expected to be difficult to complete, there are a number of ways to mitigate this in a survey.

Imagine a task that represents a single step in a larger process, such as entering payment information during an online checkout. If participants are not able to complete the step, the script should describe how to proceed so they can continue with the following tasks or steps in the task.

If the UX researcher feels that there is a real chance that participants won't be able to complete a task, then the script can help mitigate these negative feelings. The following list contains some helpful advice to bear in mind:

- When the task is introduced to the participant, restate that "we are not testing you"; "task completion is the goal, but it's ok if you can't complete the task".
- Provide the participant with a timeout time. This is the maximum time a participant should spend on trying to complete the task.

Complex tasks

Complex tasks are very suitable for survey-based studies. Because there is no need to think aloud, the participant can focus on the task and easily refer back to the task instructions to make sure that they understand the task they are completing. Once the task is completed, the participant can take their time reflecting on the task and writing down their experience.

Long tasks

In a survey-based approach, it is straightforward to divide long tasks into subtasks. If, for instance, detailed feedback is desired on the first step of a check-in process, then the subtask can instruct the participant to only fill out the first step and then answer questions before getting instructions to continue.

Goal-oriented tasks

The task is much better understood if it has a goal that the participant can relate to. For instance, *Winter is coming and you are looking for a winter coat for yourself.*

Post-task questions

Post-task questions will vary based on the task and what the UX researcher is attempting to learn from the participant's experience.

Common post-task questions include the following:

- **Ability to complete the task**: "Were you able to complete the task?"
- **Ease of completing the task**: "How easy or difficult was it to complete the task?"
- **When a task was difficult to complete**: "Please explain your answer."

- **Confident**: "How confident or not confident are you that you successfully....?"
- **If exploring for pain points**: "If you were using this product outside of this study, how likely would you be to continue?"

Time-on-task measurement

Measuring the time spent by the participant to complete a task is not entirely reliable in the survey-based approach. Even though survey tools can measure the time taken or provide buttons for the participants to start and end a timer, it is not possible to see whether the participant was interrupted during the task, or to determine at which point the participant considered the task as begun or ended. As such, for survey-based studies, we prefer to ask how much time the participant subjectively believed the task took them to complete. Bear in mind, however, that people might complete a task within a couple of minutes and may subjectively perceive it to be too long, while others might think it went very quickly. Ultimately, the measurement of the subjective perception might even be a better measurement of the time spent on the task than the objective, actual time taken.

Post-session questions

Post-session questions elicit feedback based on the participant's experience throughout the study, not just for a single task. These questions start with "Based on your experience with the product during this UX study...".

Questions can include benchmark scores, such as USERindex, as discussed in `Chapter 2`, *What Not to Forget When Planning Your Study*, as well as feedback questions, such as the following:

- "What did you like most?'
- "What did you like least about the app?"
- "Was anything missing? If you could make recommendations for new features, what would they be?"

We like to ask both how likely a participant is to use the product in the future and how likely they are to recommend it to others. While these are similar questions, the qualitative feedback is often different and insightful. If appropriate, asking whether participants have used the product (or a similar product) in the past can be a more reliable indicator of future use.

End the survey by thanking the participants and allowing them to provide feedback about the study or the product. Participants often use this opportunity to reiterate something they feel strongly about or something they feel was underrepresented during the study, and it allows them to summarize their experience.

What makes for a good question?

In a remote unmoderated setting, the script is the main (and often only) way to provide information to the study participant. The script must be comprehensive, coherent, informative, and easy to understand, yet it should also be as concise as possible. Maintaining this balance can be challenging.

The saying "garbage in, garbage out" applies here; if the question is poorly formulated, the answers will be subpar. To get great insights, great questions are a necessity.

What is the desired answer?

A good question is a question that empowers participants to provide useful answers. Some things to consider when crafting a question are as follows:

- What does the question try to answer?
- How detailed does the answer have to be?
- Should the answer be a data point that answers "what" the metric is, or should it be qualitative feedback that illustrates "why" a metric is as it is?

Questions are crafted based on the preceding considerations, not based on what functionality they cover.

As an example, questions about site registration likely aim to understand whether users are able to register successfully and with ease. The question could be a simple yes/no question, and the results could be that "87% of 22 participants were able to register". This information might be sufficient in some cases, but it is unclear why 13% were not able to register, and there is no indication of how easy or difficult it was to register.

Different questions can be used to get different levels of detail, as shown in the following table:

Question	Answer Options	Sample Answer
Were you able to register?	Yes No	"Yes"
Were you able to register?	Yes No, because…	"No, because I could not enter my street number"
Rate the task of registering: Followed by Please explain your answer:	Unable to complete the task Very difficult Somewhat difficult Neither difficult nor easy Somewhat easy Very easy	"Somewhat difficult. I tried…"

Crafting the right question

One question per question

Each question tries to answer only one thing. Avoid questions like "Was the food hot and fresh when you picked it up?" The concepts "fresh" and "hot" are not the same. The food could have been considered fresh (that is, the meat or veggies looked fresh), but not hot.

Avoiding leading questions

The formulation of the question should not suggest the desired answer. This is called a leading question. Instead of asking "Were you extremely satisfied…?", the question should rather be "How satisfied or unsatisfied were you…?".

Meeting the goals

The results of the study can only be relevant to the study sponsor if they find answers to the questions they were asking. We like to document the goals in the study design and make it part of what the stakeholders review and approve. When designing the survey, we regularly ask ourselves whether the responses will help answer the study sponsor's questions. For example, asking outright what the participant thinks about a banner ad will not answer the question of whether they would have noticed it if they hadn't been directed towards it.

Clarity

Unmoderated studies are especially useful in global contexts. In order to ensure that every participant understands the questions regardless of what language the survey is in and what their native language is, the questions should use very simple, straightforward language.

Tone

The script is the main way to build rapport with the participants. The tone should be friendly and address the participant demographics, if relevant. For instance, a script aimed at children should use simple words and sentence structure, while a script aimed at non-technical users should avoid using technical terms.

Unblocking participants

It is possible that a participant is not able to complete a task, yet a subsequent task may depend on the completion of said task. The survey must account for this situation and give the participant the instructions to continue once they indicate that they were not able to complete the task. Survey tools offer branching logic to implement the different paths.

Providing clear anchors

Whenever possible, use annotated images to avoid ambiguity. For example, when asking which version of a screen the users prefer, be sure to use labeled screenshots, allowing the user to compare and also easily identify which image is associated with which label. This is also useful when asking users what they think a given symbol might represent without having to textually describe which symbol the study is referring to.

Providing a clear starting point for each task

The task description must clearly indicate how or where to start the task. Stakeholders often adopt an internal naming system to refer to pages within the product. These names are not always clear to outsiders who have no knowledge of the product. Instead of using these naming conventions, a task should include the URL, if applicable, or a screenshot of the page or screen to ensure that all participants understand where to start a task.

If a subsequent task is included in the scope, it is important that you make sure that all participants start the task at the correct location. This may be especially relevant if the previous task was difficult to complete, and participants may not all be at the same point in the interface. Providing the URL or screenshot again will ensure that the user feedback refers to the same page or action.

Facilitating sentiment expression

When asking subjective opinions, consider offering sentiment expression as a choice, with the options of "Mostly negative, because:" and "Mostly positive, because:". We do this to avoid having to interpret sentiment into the response. A participant's response might be full of negative items even though their overall sentiment is mostly positive.

After completing a task, we like asking how/why the participant knows that he has actually successfully completed the task. This usually provides some insight into how well the product communicates.

Follow-up questions

When writing the survey questions, it is important to imagine the range of possible responses. For example, the question "Did you consult the manual when setting up the device?" will probably lead the study sponsors to immediately ask in which cases this was necessary. Therefore, a natural follow-up question would be "For which tasks did you consult the manual?". Other subsequent questions could be whether the manual helped the participant complete the task, and/or whether the participant usually consults the manual. As there is no opportunity to come up with these questions on the fly in a survey-based UX study, they need to be considered when writing the survey.

Obvious questions

It is bad practice to ask superfluous, obvious questions, such as "Where would you click to check out your shopping cart?" when there is a huge **Check out your shopping cart** button in the middle of the screen. These kinds of questions can make the participants feel annoyed for having to state the obvious, or worse, they might think that the question is so easy that there must be another correct response to the question that they have not discovered.

Preparing for the study

Once the script has been crafted and added in a survey tool, there are just a few more things to check before starting the study.

Dry run

- Check the product under testing to make sure that participants can access it. This includes checking the URL, credentials, or the installation of an executable.
- Run through the script to confirm the following:
    - The instructions contain all the necessary information.
    - The tasks follow a logical sequence.
    - The right question type has been used to get the intended type of results.
    - The session time estimate is accurate.
    - Any branching is correctly configured.
- If the study is a team effort, then make sure that one person is appointed as the main point of contact. This person should be available to follow the progress of the sessions and be ready to jump in should participants have questions.

Scheduling participants

Once participants have been recruited as described in Chapter 3, *How to Effectively Recruit Participants*, scheduling is pretty straightforward. Participants need access to the script. The script, in turn, includes all the necessary information for the participants to execute the study.

Even though participants have been vetted for the study, have been notified of it, and have confirmed their participation, some participants will not complete the study for one reason or another. It is possible to invite the exact number of participants and only add more participants when it becomes clear how many participants are not completing the study. This approach will possibly reduce the total reward or compensation that must be paid out, but it can take a bit longer to get all the submissions. Alternatively, more participants than required can be invited at the onset in order to make up for any potential no-shows with the consequence that there might also be more submissions.

Running the study

As mentioned previously, the study will run itself, since the participants have all the necessary information to complete the session. As the submissions come in, the UX researcher can do a quick review to ensure that the participants completed the session as expected and provided meaningful comments.

If the results are not as insightful as was expected, there may be an opportunity to go back to the study participant and ask them to elaborate. If a follow-up is possible and desired, it is best to do this as soon as possible so that the study participants still have their experience fresh in their minds.

Next steps

Once the sessions are completed, the raw results are available for the UX researcher to analyze. We will deep dive into the subject of analysis later in this book.

While the goal of every study is to answer the questions the study sponsor specified for the product, it is useful to keep a question bank of survey questions by industry. Some industries have user journeys that are more uniform than others. We have found that a question bank for e-commerce, such as an online checkout or online ordering, can be reused, to a large extent.

Summary

Remote unmoderated studies using surveys are a great way to gather user feedback that is both quick and deep. They are a viable solution for running usability tests with geographically dispersed participants in their natural environment, using their own devices according to their own schedule, while requiring less effort from the UX researcher (but more skill in survey creation).

A hybrid approach of user videos and surveys can be an excellent option as well. The next chapter describes the details of hybrid remote unmoderated studies.

7
Running a Remote Unmoderated Study with a Hybrid Approach

As we mentioned in Chapter 1, *Why Everyone Should Run Remote Usability Tests*, in a remote unmoderated usability study, the UX researcher sets up the UX study and analyzes the results, but unlike a moderated study, the participants complete the session without a moderator present. This allows the study participants to complete the study tasks where and when it is most natural to them. An unmoderated study using the hybrid approach uses a combination of the survey and user video methods that were introduced in the previous chapters. Participants create user videos and answer survey questions.

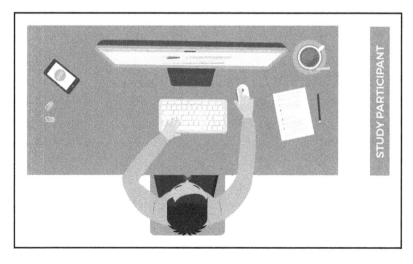

Hybrid remote unmoderated study

An advantage of this method is that it provides user videos showing what the participant did, as well as self-reported feedback. It is also relatively lightweight and has a quick turnaround.

As with any unmoderated method, the challenges of this method include the inability to ask follow-up questions, as is possible in moderated studies.

The major UX research efforts in unmoderated studies include the following:

- Planning the study
- Recruiting and managing the participants
- Writing the script
- Analyzing the data and writing the report

As this is a combination of two methods, most of what applies to either method also applies to the hybrid of the two. This chapter will, therefore, highlight where the hybrid approach may be different from what we described in the previous chapters on user video and survey-based methodologies.

About the hybrid method

The hybrid method combines the survey method with user videos. It is our preferred method because the survey questions provide in-depth, self-reported feedback while the user videos allow for observation of the users' experiences.

Strengths of the hybrid method

The main advantage of this approach is the combination of user videos and self-reported feedback. This results in richer information than what would have been available in survey-only or video-only studies.

Self-reported data informed by user videos

Because of the limitations of self-reported data, we often recommend collecting user videos as a secondary source to investigate areas of concern. When reviewing the user videos, the UX researcher can form their own opinion of the user experience. We recently had an instance in a survey-based study where a participant reported that they were able to complete the task and provided no further written feedback. It was debatable whether the task was indeed completed successfully since the system did not successfully record the registration. Perhaps an error occurred which the user did not notice because its display was too subtle or he clicked away too fast. A user video could have helped identify the issue.

Device and product version confirmation

A user video is the visual proof that the participant used a specific device or version of the product. For instance, we've had issues in survey-based unmoderated studies where we received strange results, only to find out that a participant had accidentally used the live instead of the development version of a product. A user video would have made it very easy to confirm this.

Reducing fraud

As we mentioned in the previous chapter, one of the drawbacks of the survey method is that it is not always easy to verify whether a participant exercised due diligence in completing the tasks. A user video in combination with the survey method provides visual proof of this.

Limitations of the hybrid method

The same limitations we discussed in previous chapters are applicable here as well. An additional limitation is the increased effort compared to either the video or the survey approach.

Increased analysis effort for the UX researcher

The UX researcher must analyze the self-reported survey responses as well as the user videos. This is obviously more time-consuming than only reviewing survey results or only reviewing user videos. The multiple data streams, including quantitative data, self-reported feedback, and the user videos, create a rich set of data to investigate and extract findings from.

Study organization

The study must be organized based on the session duration, the number of participants, and the tasks.

Session duration

We feel comfortable running hybrid studies with 45 to 60 minute sessions, a similar duration to the survey-based approach. The duration may be roughly the same, but there are fewer tasks in the hybrid study in order to account for the extra participant effort providing both video and written feedback.

Number of participants

In order to make efficient use of the UX researcher's time, the number of participants for hybrid method studies usually falls between the typical numbers for video-based and survey-based approaches. We often settle on 12 to 15 participants.

Number of tasks

The recommended number of tasks is again related to the planned session duration, but it should ideally be less than in a survey-based study because of the overhead of the video recording.

The script

The UX researcher creates the script based on their conversations with the stakeholders about the main areas to be covered. The script is provided to the study participants at the start of the study and should include the following:

- Introduction
- Instructions
- Tasks
- Post-task questions
- Post-session questions

A sample script is provided in the appendix.

Introduction

The introduction should include the following:

- A thank-you for participating.
- A description of what will happen in the session.
- An explanation that the goal is to get honest user feedback, and that there are no right or wrong answers.
- A listing of any limitations, such as whether the product under testing is a test version or a prototype. Inform the participant of this and the possible consequences: There may be bugs, not all links will necessarily work, content may be missing, replaced by placeholders, incoherent, and so on.
- A confirmation of the expected schedule, including how much time the participant has to complete the session and the expected amount of user effort.
- A contact email address and name in case participants have questions.

Instructions

The instructions explain how to properly execute the think-aloud and write-down-what-you-think protocols and how to record user videos, and should cover the guidelines that relate to logistics, such as the devices and software to be used.

Standalone responses

The participants should be instructed to refrain from referring to their previous written responses while recording the user video and vice versa—they should not, in the written responses, refer to their user videos. Ideally, each video and each written response can be taken on its own without further need to correlate it with another piece of data.

Further instructions are discussed in depth in the *Instructions* section of the chapters on user videos and surveys respectively. A sample hybrid script can be found in the appendix.

Tasks

The same guidelines for task writing from the previous chapters are relevant for hybrid methods as well.

Recording start and end

In a hybrid study, where video recording and written responses are intermixed, the task description must be very clear on when the recording should start and when it should end. For example, in a music-streaming application, if the task to be recorded is the retrieval of one's personal favorites, then the task instructions should explicitly state that the participant should record until they are displaying their favorites on the screen, at which point they can end the recording and respond to the subsequent questions.

Balance between open questions and user videos

Both open questions and user videos are great for extracting unguided feedback from the participants. However, both require a certain amount of time, and if they are requested for the same task, the participant might feel that they are merely repeating what they thought out loud for the video as a written response to the open question. It is therefore important to find the right balance between open questions and videos, with little or no overlap.

User videos for relevant tasks only

Given that combining user videos with a survey puts some extra strain on the participant, we try to limit the user videos to those tasks where it makes sense. If a task is very short and straightforward, such as logging in to a website, it may not make sense to ask the participant for a user video.

Similarly, if the task has multiple steps, and survey questions are best asked after each step, a user video may not make sense. Limiting the number of user videos not only helps the participants, but it also reduces the effort for the UX researcher.

In some cases, we make user videos optional. This may be helpful when a target user profile is difficult to recruit for, as it allows those who don't feel comfortable with recording user videos to participate in the study anyway.

Post-task or post-session questions

Chapter 6, *Running a Remote Unmoderated Study with a Survey*, focuses on survey-based remote unmoderated studies and provides a close analysis of survey question types.

Writing tips

The writing tips outlined in the previous chapters apply here as well.

Since the script needs to cover both user videos and survey questions, it will be longer than a script for one of the other methods. Keeping the language simple and being concise is even more important in this case.

Preparing for the study

Once the tasks have been created and the script has been crafted, there are just a few more things to check before starting the study:

- Check the product under testing to make sure that participants can access it. This includes checking the URL, credentials, or the installation of an executable.
- Check that the script contains all necessary information.
- Do a dry run of the tasks to confirm the following:
    - Tasks are clear and presented in logical order—for instance, registering should precede logging in
    - Questions make sense and use the correct question type
    - The time required to complete the session is within the expected parameters and is correctly reflected in the script

Scheduling participants

Scheduling the participants does not differ much from the previous chapters. Here too, it is recommended that you recruit additional participants in order to have backup should there be no-shows in the original set of participants.

Running the study

As with all unmoderated studies, it is important to keep track of the responses as they come in in order to be able to react quickly, if necessary.

Next steps

Once the sessions are completed, the user videos and survey answers must be available to the UX researcher and any other team members for review and analysis.

Summary

If given the choice, remote unmoderated hybrid studies are always our preference, because we get the best of both worlds (of the remote unmoderated studies). We receive self-reported user feedback and we can view how participants interact with a product. With the added advantage of being easily rolled out globally and less restraining from a scheduling perspective, this method definitely holds its own in comparison with the remote moderated method.

In Chapter 8, *What to Consider When Analyzing and Presenting the Study Results*, we will look into the analysis and presentation of remote study results.

8
What to Consider When Analyzing and Presenting the Study Results

Once the study has been completed, the analysis of the data begins. We do not recommend skipping this analysis because it helps in creating the big picture across all participants, and puts their user feedback in perspective.

Analyzing the data

In order to efficiently analyze the data, we recommend first preparing the raw data and then compiling the results before diving into the analysis.

Preparing the raw data

The raw data is the starting point for the analysis, but that raw data comes in different formats for the different types of studies we are covering in this book.

Remote moderated studies

As this type of study is usually recorded, ideally the sessions should be transcribed. This is especially recommended when the number of participants is larger, the scope of the study more extensive, and the agreed deliverable requires this level of detail. A transcription service will provide a written version of what is said during the session, preferably timestamped. They are very useful because they allow the UX researcher to access specific content more efficiently than they would by navigating within the actual recordings. They also provide the researcher with the ability to search through the session using keywords.

So the raw data for the analysis of remote moderated studies will typically comprise the participant profiles, the UX researcher's notes, the session transcripts, and optionally, post-session questionnaires. If there were observers and the observers took notes, then these notes can also be part of the raw data.

Remote unmoderated studies with videos

The starting point for unmoderated studies with videos is the videos themselves.

The raw data for the analysis of this type of study is, therefore, typically the participant profiles, the videos, and optionally, post-session questionnaires.

Remote unmoderated studies with surveys

This is the easiest variant in terms of preparation of raw data for analysis because the survey responses will be the sole source for this type of study, assuming that the participant demographic information was also gathered as part of the survey.

Hybrid remote unmoderated studies

The hybrid studies are a combination of the video and survey-based methodologies and thus the raw data comprises both the user videos as well as the survey responses.

One important thing to note concerning all the data gathered is that any personal information provided by the participant during any type of study should be treated (that is, it should be removed or made illegible) in order to ensure that it is not part of the deliverables for the study. Personal information comprises the participants' names, email addresses, and any information they may have inadvertently shared, such as their credentials (given when logging into applications) or banking data (given when testing banking apps), for example.

Compiling the findings

The next step is to compile the findings so that they can be analyzed easily. The findings can be organized per participant, but it is better to do this per task, as this gives a more holistic view of how well or badly the task was mastered across all participants. If, however, there are any particularities that relate to a specific participant profile attribute, then this should be highlighted.

When analyzing the results of a hybrid study, we like to first view all the video data before looking into the survey responses. It is not mandatory to use this order, but we feel that it gives us a good overview of the feedback before we dive into the written data.

Observed or recorded data

In order to more easily identify patterns, it is useful to organize the data from the user videos and the moderated studies in tables, listing qualitative information such as the following:

- Issues the users encountered
- Situations where the participant said *probably*, *I believe*, or similar words expressing that they weren't confident
- Things the study participants felt strongly about, whether negative or positive
- Responses to open-ended questions

We also similarly organize useful quantitative information, such as the following:

- Whether the task was completed successfully
- The time taken to complete the task
- The number of errors encountered
- Post-session questionnaire responses

If the study sponsor does not wish that quantitative data be reported on, it can be omitted. We have encountered customers who specifically asked not to report on any quantitative data for moderated or unmoderated studies with videos because they view such studies as purely qualitative, and were therefore not interested in the quantitative results.

Videos can be watched with a faster playback speed of 1.25x or 1.5x to make their analysis more efficient. At 1.5x, a 10-minute user video will take just over 6.5 minutes to watch. When watching only one video, this does not seem to be a large time saver, but it quickly becomes significant when analyzing all the videos created during the study.

Self-reported data

For studies with surveys, all the required information is available in the raw data of the survey responses. Many survey tools offer text-analysis tools for the analysis of qualitative user feedback, and most survey tools provide an option to export the responses in a table format.

If the raw data is the agreed study deliverable, then this data can be grouped (by participant profile, device used, or other criteria) and color coded (yes/no responses and Likert scale ratings, for example, can be given appropriate colors) in order to make it more digestible.

Interpreting the findings

Now the best part begins: diving into the data and making sense of it. We work our way through the raw data, task by task (or question by question).

At this point, we are actually already compiling the report. For each task that we analyze, we directly enter the findings into the report and start building it. We like doing it like this because we (the authors of this book) both appreciate efficiency and hate repeating work. UX researchers can, of course, separate the analysis step from the report-compilation step, if this makes more sense to them.

Visualising the data

The first step is to create a graph that visualizes the results. Visualization is better for identifying patterns and potential outliers than sifting through textual data.

We recommend using common graph types that allow the viewers to focus on the data and not occupy themselves with how best to read the chart. The best visualization depends on the type of question and thus the type of responses gathered. There are many good books written on this topic, and we do not intend to make this book about data visualization, so the following sections will provide a brief overview of the chart types we use most.

(Stacked) column/bar chart

A column or bar chart represents the frequency distribution of categorical data. The heights or lengths of the columns or bars are proportional to the frequencies of the categories:

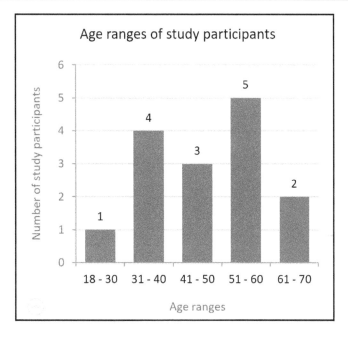

Column chart

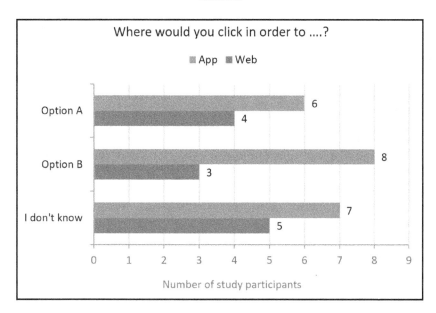

Bar chart

A stacked column or bar chart is similar to a regular column or bar chart, except that, in addition, each column or bar represents a whole and the segments of the column or bar represent different categories of that whole. They have the advantage that they take up less space, but may be less legible for colorblind readers if color is used to distinguish the individual segments:

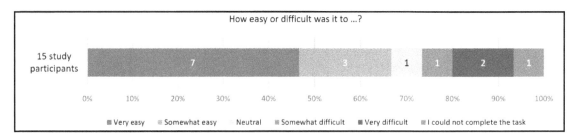

Stacked bar chart

Column/bar charts are best used for representing responses to multiple-choice questions, whether they have single or multiple answers, such as how often the study participants go grocery shopping, or Likert scale rating questions. They can also be used to display the response to an open question when those responses do not vary too much, and can be summarized with a succinct word or short phrase—for example, 'where would you click in order to…?". They are our go-to choice for representing discrete information.

Stacked column/bar charts are best used for Likert scale rating questions or single-answer questions, such as those with the binary response of "yes" or "no". They also make it easy to determine the top box score—that is, the sum of the percentages of the top two most favorable ratings.

When there are more than six categories, or when the category labels are relatively long and a horizontal layout would benefit the legibility of the chart, it is better to use a bar chart instead of a column chart.

Line chart

A line chart represents information as a series of data points connected by straight line segments. The line chart can also be drawn using only markers when the lines might suggest a trend that is not relevant.

Line charts are best used for displaying the responses to a semantic differential scale question, as shown in the following chart:

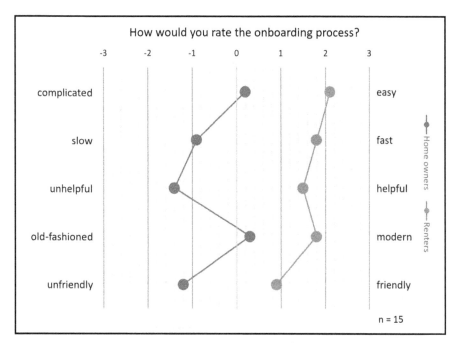

Line chart

Pie chart

A pie chart illustrates the numerical proportion of categorical data by dividing a circular chart into sectors (or slices). The size of each slice—or more specifically, the length of the arc of a slice—represents the frequency of the category.

When the center of the pie chart is cut out, this is then called a doughnut chart, as shown in the following chart:

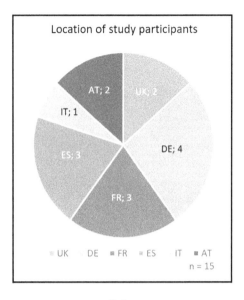

Pie chart

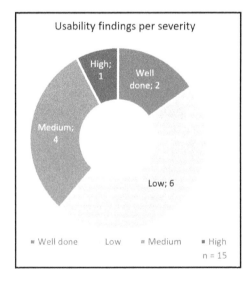

Doughnut chart

This chart is best used when only a few categories are to be displayed, or when the exact proportions are less important than the high-level impression. This is because it is more difficult to discern the relative sizes of the slices when the chart depicts many categories. If used, we recommend to always provide data labels for the slices that include both the category name as well as the numerical value or a percentage—for example, "North, 28%" instead of just "North".

Table

Sometimes, a simple table is the best way to lay out information. We often use tables to display the responses to matrix questions, such as ranking or grouping questions.

In order to easily identify the top winners or losers (if losers are of interest) or the most mentioned values, we often color code the cells and/or make the text bold, as shown in the following table:

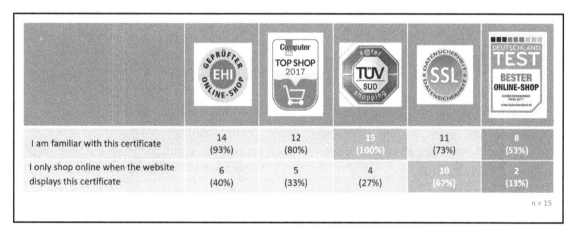

Table for a matrix question

Word cloud

A word cloud is a visual display of the words in a qualitative dataset, organized by the frequency of their use. Generally, the larger a word is displayed, the more frequently it was found in the response data. Most word cloud generators can be configured to exclude counting supporting words, such as articles, pronouns, and so on. This is best used when the responses are simple words or short phrases. A word cloud can also be used to display the responses to multi-answer questions when the actual numerical value is less relevant than the tendency the data expresses.

The following image shows a word cloud of the qualitative responses to a question:

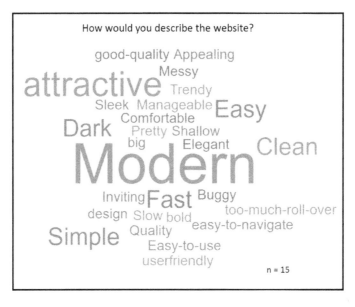

Word cloud

Lists

Lists are also a very simple way of representing response information. They are best used for open questions, such as "what is your first impression of …?". They can be used for both unclustered and clustered responses:

- **Unclustered responses**:
  - For remote moderated studies where the number of responses might be relatively low, the responses can be listed verbatim, ideally enclosed by quotes to support the understanding that these are verbatim statements.
  - For a more visual display, the responses can also be enclosed in a speech bubble, with an optional badge to enable a quick visual identification of the ratio of negative to positive responses. This is useful when the responses are phrases or complete sentences, as shown in the following screenshot:

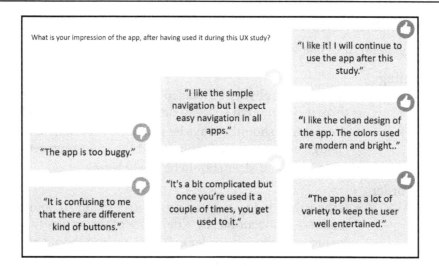

What is your impression of the app, after having used it during this UX study?

"I like it! I will continue to use the app after this study."

"I like the simple navigation but I expect easy navigation in all apps."

"I like the clean design of the app. The colors used are modern and bright.."

"The app is too buggy."

"It is confusing to me that there are different kind of buttons."

"It's a bit complicated but once you're used it a couple of times, you get used to it."

"The app has a lot of variety to keep the user well entertained."

List of unclustered responses

- **Clustered responses**:
  - When there are many responses, it might make sense to cluster the responses in order to more easily identify the family of topics the responses belong to.
  - In this case, we list the common theme for a group of responses, list how many responses belong to this grouping, and add one or two verbatim responses to illustrate this, as shown in the following screenshot:

What did you like most about the app?

Design. "the design"; "the modern look"; "the colors"; "the fresh look" (8 mentions)

Ease-of-use. "it was so simple to complete the task"; "super easy to use"; "searching was so easy" (4 mentions)

Navigation. "I didn't have to think. Everything was where I expected it"; "everything can be reached via the nav bar" (3 mentions)

n = 15

List of clustered responses

Best practices when representing data

Here are some general rules that help make graphs more legible:

- **Labeling**:
    - Axes should always be labeled or a legend should be provided if there is not enough space to display the value labels along the axes.
    - A chart title should always be provided especially if there is not enough context to easily infer what the chart represents.
    - Type fonts and sizes should be easily legible.

- **Sort order**:
    - If the values being counted can be ordered in an obvious manner—for example, by a daily, monthly, or yearly frequency—then the order on the chart axis should reflect this.
    - If the values do not have any obvious logical order—for example, if we were looking at the most-used online payment methods—then the chart will be easier to read if the bars are ordered according to the numerical value.
    - Where applicable, categories should be sorted according to their order in the survey question—for example, from most negative to most positive or vice versa.

- **Use of color**:
    - If the values displayed in the chart can be expressed in meaningful colors, such as green for "yes", red for "no", and grey for "I don't know", then this makes the chart easier to consume. Of course, this only makes sense if the report is targeted at people whose culture gives these colors the same meaning. Otherwise, neutral colors should be used.
    - When colors do not bring additional value, we either use a variety of colors, avoiding those that might have an associated meaning—such as red or green—or use only one color.
    - It is important to be mindful that colorblind people might not be able to discern the different colors used, and as such, they should not be the only means to convey that information. Fill patterns can also be used, and of course, everything should be appropriately labeled, as shown in the following graph:

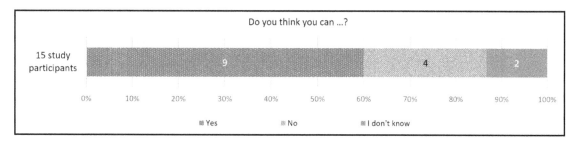

Stacked bar chart using colors and fill patterns

- **Choice of axes**:
    - When one of the dimensions is time, the column chart should be used and the time dimension should be plotted on the horizontal axis in ascending order from left to right.
    - The frequency axis should always start at 0.

Identifying issues

Once the data has been nicely laid out graphically, the UX researcher can use it to identify the issues the participants encountered. Analyzing the study results is exciting because the UX researcher gets to view the interface from the perspective of each of the participants and their unique situation. It is impossible to describe exactly how to do this, as it will vary from study to study (because it depends on the goals, the tasks completed, and the questions asked), but here are some pointers on how to go about it.

Use the following questions to uncover issues encountered by the study participants during the study execution. For each issue, note the number of participants that encountered it, and, where relevant or possible, whether a particular profile was more affected than the others. Certain profile-related questions can be relevant when analyzing the results. This includes the version of the product that the participant used for testing and their device and/or browser specifics.

Where did the study participants struggle with a task?

The difficulty of a task can be seen in the ease-of-use rating or task completion scores. Look into the reasons that the participants gave, determine how many participants encountered the same issue, and identify whether there is an underlying issue. For larger numbers of participants, it might also be of interest to look into the participant profiles for similarities, such as "participants familiar with competitive products found this task to be …".

Where did the participants voice (or respond with) insecurity?

When participants use phrases such as *I believe...* or *probably...*, that usually indicates that the participant might not have been entirely confident that they were completing the task correctly.

Were there any big emotions, whether negative or positive?

A participant may have successfully completed a task, and may even have rated it as being somewhat easy to complete while still voicing very negative opinions about it. This may be because the participant finds the steps to complete the task easy enough, but overall thinks that there are too many steps, or that they have to enter data that they do not want to enter, and so on. It is important to analyze these types of discrepancies in order to validate that the rating is correct and better understand the user feedback.

It is always nice to report positive findings, and the best starting place for these findings are responses from participants where they were particularly positive. These are also findings, albeit not *issues*.

Are there any outliers?

A finding that is observed with only one participant (or a similarly small number of participants) is considered an outlier. How to deal with such responses will depend on whether the participant is representative of the target user, whether other participants might have encountered the same issue but did not notice it, and other such factors.

Are participants consistently using different terminology?

If the participants are consistently using different terminology than that which is used on the product, the product might not be immediately understandable.

Are there any inconsistencies in the responses?

This is especially pertinent in survey-based studies where no follow up is possible. We have encountered participants that responded to all USERindex questions (positively formulated statements) with "strongly disagree" while at the same time rating the product under testing with five stars and responding to the NPS question (how likely are you to recommend this product...?) with a ten (extremely likely). We have also had responses where participants rated a task as difficult, but who in their elaboration stated that "it was not at all difficult, because....".

What to do then? If possible, the best course of action is to follow up with the participant and validate the responses. In a remote unmoderated study using surveys, this might not always be possible, in which case, it might be necessary to exclude the response from the evaluation of the question

Were there any "false positives"?

False positives are cases where a participant completes the task, and finds it easy to do so, but actually completed it wrong or completed another task without having any clue that it was wrong. If the task was completed wrongly without the study participant being aware of it, then this is a usability issue that needs to be reported on, whereas if the study participant erroneously completed another task, then those responses need to be excluded from the report. The latter has happened to us when a study participant called up the live website of the product under testing instead of using the prototype link provided to them, for example, or where the staging environment had links to the production site and the participants inadvertently ended up there.

Did anyone encounter bugs?

We would be the first to step up and emphatically state that a UX study is not Quality Assurance, which is aimed at finding bugs, but how the product under testing recovers from a defect is quite interesting from a usability perspective. We had a participant once who struggled for ten minutes, unsuccessfully trying and retrying to enter her email address in a web form. Eventually, it worked and she continued with the task thinking that she had done something wrong. She hadn't. There was a bug in the website that made the entry of the email address work intermittently.

At this point, the analysis per task will have been completed, and a list of issues has been compiled and, optionally, qualified by participant profile, frequency of occurrence, and so on. Often, for remote moderated UX studies, for example, the UX researcher can use the aforementioned questions to prepare an informal report with the most important findings. We recommend clearly marking the report as *interim*.

Identifying recommendations

The goal of any usability study is not to simply list the identified issues while observing users performing tasks with the product under testing. Ideally, the results will also comprise recommendations on how to improve on or even eliminate the identified issues. This is where the skill of the UX researcher is most important (well, second maybe to the script or survey writing at the beginning of a project). Not every negative remark made by a participant during the study is necessarily an issue that requires remediation.

The recommendations are not an exact reflection of the issues encountered by the study participants. Instead, the UX researcher might exclude an issue because it is too specific to a participant and they might include a remediation recommendation for an issue that none of the participants stumbled over.

We are sometimes asked not to provide recommendations as part of the deliverables of a UX study. It has happened when a customer wanted their own design department to determine remediation solutions that they deemed feasible, for example, or when the in-house UX staff wanted to identify both the issues and remediations themselves.

The task of the UX researcher is to parse the findings and, using their experience, known best practices, and standards, to first determine which findings should be considered issues, rate how severe the issue is, and provide one or more remediation recommendations.

The following are some recommendations for writing useful and useable recommendations partially taken from the article **Recommendations on Recommendations: Making usability usable** (`http://uxpamagazine.org/making_usability_usable/`), and extended with our own recommendations.

Make recommendations constructive and direct

It's hard being on the receiving end of what is essentially criticism of the current design. We've been there too, so we try to formulate recommendations constructively. We never just list an issue—we also explain why it is an issue and provide at least one remediation suggestion.

Provide detail and illustrate

Detail helps to provide context. If the issue occurs in a specific constellation, it needs to be explained; if it occurs over multiple screen steps, that needs to be illustrated, all while staying concise and to the point. We like to add images or video clips where available because a visual explanation is often easier to understand than pure text.

Address only the original usability problem

A UX study is about UX, and not about how to best support business goals or improve marketing copy. When kicking off a UX study, this type of goal might be listed as the aim of the study, but as we elaborated in `Chapter 2`, *What Not to Forget When Planning Your Study*, they are not valid UX goals, and might be better served using another tool. Do not provide visual design, product marketing, or coding recommendations; recommendations should be restricted to usability and interaction design.

Speak the readers' language

This is usability 101: use the language of your target audience. We have this recommendation in many of our studies when a company exposes their internal, very specific jargon to their customers/users. The report of a UX study is no different. It is very often targeted at non-UX professionals and as such should use language that everyone will understand.

Provide alternatives

A recommendation should always list the easiest change that will bring about an improvement. But we do like to, additionally, list alternatives that might not be as easy to implement, but would bring about even greater improvement. The ideal solution may be clearly expensive and potentially not even on the product roadmap yet, such as offering a touchscreen interface instead of physical buttons. Often, less expensive solutions are thinkable that are less than perfect, but which can provide a quick fix. The UX researcher should list all possible remediation alternatives, highlighting which are quick, short-term fixes and which are the ideal target solutions.

Solve the problem

A great recommendation solves the problem for all users, not just for a small subset. It deals with the cause of the problem, not just the symptoms.

Assign a severity

When confronted with a bunch of recommendations for improvement, it is useful to understand which cause the user the most problems and ensure that these are addressed in a prioritized manner. In order to be able to do so, the UX researcher should assign severity levels to their recommendations.

The severity levels should take the following into consideration:

- **The frequency** (whether it happens very often or very rarely; how many participants were impacted)
- **The criticality** (what the impact is if the user is hindered by this issue)
- **The persistence** (whether the user can learn to overcome the issue or will be continuously confronted with it)

Focus on the user

A usability study is about making an interface easier to use by the user. Intraoffice politics, the potential effort involved in implementing a recommendation, and so on should not influence what the UX researcher deems an issue, or which remediation solution they suggest.

Reporting the data

Depending on what was originally agreed upon, the report may take on many forms. We will focus on the most elaborate one: the formal, written report.

Other kinds of reports may comprise a verbal briefing, an informal memo in the form of an email or a quick report in a status meeting. Other variants include not documenting the results, but instead updating the requirement documentation (in whatever form: wireframes or otherwise) or directly creating tasks for the development teams. This is very common when the UX researcher is not an external consultant, or the UX study is integrated into an iterative, agile environment.

A written report benefits from usability principles, just like any digital interface. It should be well-structured, with clear headings and making appropriate use of color and visual material. We have seen reports where charts were displayed using color, and green was used to denote failed tasks. Of course, interpretation of color depends on culture, but this was a report consumed by a Western culture.

The aim of the report is twofold:

- Its main purpose, of course, is to document the findings of the UX study and the derived recommendations
- The secondary aim is to record the study context

Participant names should not be included in the report, nor should they be deducible from the video clips (if provided as a deliverable).

Audience

The report of the results of a remote usability test will be of interest to different people within the organization that requested the study. Each group of people will be looking for different things in the report, and this, in turn, will influence how to structure the report and how to deliver the results.

The CEO will want to know what the bottom line of the test results is. The product manager will like to know how to increase conversion. The UX professionals will want to know where the users stumbled with their design. The developer will want to know if any bugs surfaced. A good report should, therefore, have a section where key facts can be easily consumed, followed by sections with more detail for those who require more data.

Content of the report

The report of the results of a remote usability test should ideally include the following elements in this order:

1. A cover page
2. A high-level summary
3. The study context
4. The findings
5. Benchmark scores
6. Improvement/remediation recommendations
7. Next steps
8. An appendix

Each section should follow the same layout principles, making it easy for the reader to quickly consume the content without having to first understand how each page is structured.

Cover page

The cover page should at the very least name the product under testing, the date of the report, and the name of the author.

Summary

The summary serves all audiences, as it gives the big picture and sets the scene. From our experience, parties interested in further detail will read on, while busy executives may stop after the summary. The summary section should, therefore, provide a condensed version of the results of the test. This is easier said than done. What information should be included? What is potentially too detailed?

The goal(s)

A good place to start is the goal of the test. What were the reasons for running the usability test? Ideally, this information was provided at the start of the project and guided the entire execution. In a sentence or two, address how the objectives were met. For example, if an objective was to validate the navigation concept of a new app, the summary statement should say how easy or difficult the study participants found it to navigate the app, and whether there were extreme blockers.

Any critical issues

Any issues of critical severity that were identified during the study should be listed, even if they do not necessarily align with an objective.

The bottom line

A one-statement summary is often very useful. We have found that rounding the summary up with one statement that either states that the digital product was generally well received or generally not well received helps set the expectation for the rest of the report.

Optional details

The summary can also contain an overview of the number of recommendations and their severity, as well as listing the benchmark scores measured. Or an overview comparison of the top box ease-of-use or satisfaction scores for the tasks completed during the study. Alternatively, a high-level overview of the most important positive and negative findings can be listed. It all depends on what best represents the answer to the goals of the study.

We usually write the summary last after documenting everything else. This allows us to walk through all the participant responses/observations and identify the main issues that caused the most problems.

Study context

The next section describes the context of the study. This comprises the following:

- Metadata about the study, such as when the study was completed, how many participants took part, what the goals of the study were, who the UX researcher was and so on
- A short description of the methodology used
- The name of the product that was tested, and in what version it was tested
- The number and duration of sessions (for remote moderated studies)
- Relevant demographic information about the study participants (age, gender, location, and so on)
- Further characteristics of the study participants (such as the device used, previous experience with the product under testing, and so on)

Where the study context section is placed in the report depends on the audience. If the audience is less interested in these details, it can be placed at the end of the report as an appendix.

Benchmark scores

Benchmark scores will help the organization understand how their digital product measures up to other similar products, or to previous studies that were run with the same product.

If available, it is always helpful to provide industry-specific benchmark scores or scores from previous products or studies as a reference that will help interpret the values achieved in the current study.

Findings

The findings are one of the core sections of the report. As the report will be available to many different people with varying interests, it is important to provide the findings in a manner that will cater to each group. We have found that it helps to provide the following for each task completed or question asked:

- A visualization of the results in the form of a chart, where possible

- A statement summing up the bottom line, along the lines of "78% of the 15 participants found it easy or very easy to complete the task" (we like to use percentages, but are aware that they may suggest a statistical significance that is mostly not given with the typically small number of participants in a remote study, and therefore we always explicitly state the number of participants)
- Some additional detail, such as verbatim comments of the participants
- A screenshot of the screen in question

This structure allows the group of readers who just want to identify the bottom line to achieve this quickly by reading the summary statement, while other target groups, who might like to understand the background of the summary statement, can delve into the details. Using appropriate coloring and the same chart type for similar questions will additionally help the readers to quickly scan the report for red flags. If the organization has threshold values for ease-of-use or satisfaction scores, for example, then the report should highlight for each task or question whether the threshold value was reached or not.

Improvement/remediation recommendations

This section tells the organization what they need to focus on in order to improve the usability of their digital product. It should be prefaced or followed by a page describing the significance of the severity levels (if the recommendations have been assigned a severity level).

We like to start this section off with the things that were done well. Only focusing on the negatives can be disheartening. Then the improvement recommendations should follow, listed in order of highest to lowest severity.

Where available, the findings should be illustrated with screenshots, tables or charts, and verbatim comments or video clips. We once presented the results of a UX study and showed a video clip to underline a specific finding. The study participant on the video gave a loud, drawn-out sigh that spoke more to the audience than the textual description did. They felt his pain.

Verbatim participant comments

The voice of the user can be more powerful than just simply pointing out an issue. At this point in the analysis and presentation, the UX researcher will have a very good feel for the results and the core findings. Concluding the report with a few verbatim comments from participants that illustrate the main highlights will allow the reader of the report to hear the actual words of real users.

Conclusion and next steps

The summary usually pretty much contains the conclusion, but ending the report with a conclusion that sums up in a sentence or two what the bottom line of the results is—mostly positive, mostly negative, or somewhere in between—is an excellent segue to the suggestions for the next steps. We have mentioned this before: a usability study should not be a one-off; the goal is always to improve the product being tested, not to document its flaws. This section should therefore always state what the best next steps should be—for example, a specific user journey that the next UX study should focus on.

Appendix

The appendix is used to provide supporting material that is not necessarily part of the core content of the report.

Some of the items that can be provided here include the following:

- **Screener**: The screener questions used to recruit the participants
- **Survey questions**: The list of questions contained in the survey, if applicable
- **Session logs**: The recorded logs of each session
- **Links to the raw data**: The videos, the survey responses, and so on

Summary

The analysis and the presentation of the study results is one of the largest chunks of effort when executing a remote usability study, and it pays off when the audience can empathize with the users of the product under testing.

Now that we know how to write a report, the following chapter will look into what to do next with the study results.

Thanks! And What Now? 9

A study is essentially completed when it has been executed and the feedback has been compiled into a report (whatever form this may take). But what happens then?

We strongly recommend scheduling a debrief session with all interested parties to review the results and give the UX researcher the opportunity to explain the feedback and recommendations, as well as allow for questions. It closes the loop with the stakeholders who participated in the original kick-off session, ensuring that the value of the UX study does not go unnoticed, and it's a good forum for agreeing, as a whole, what the next steps should be with regards to the UX strategy. Ideally, a UX study is not a one-off endeavor: it is a recurring event, and previous studies feed into what future studies should cover.

The debrief session

A lot of people will roll their eyes when they hear about a debrief session and see it as a waste of time, if all it is is a debrief. We see it as much more: It is a chance to introduce the original stakeholders, as well as additional stakeholders, to the findings of the study. It's a beginning rather than an end in collaborating with design, production, marketing, and development teams.

The debrief session can be made more engaging by using a lot of visual and not too much textual material. Studies that included video recordings can be presented using a highlights reel containing the most interesting findings, or by showing short video clips illustrating the key points throughout the session.

The most enjoyable debrief sessions are those where the product under testing was a pure delight to use and the bottom line of the report is very positive. In rare cases, the study sponsors might be a bit skeptical of positive results, especially if they had specific concerns that they feel were not echoed by the participants. The UX researcher's professional evaluation can help frame the feedback from the participants and, hopefully, set the study sponsor's mind at ease.

The opposite can also happen, where a product is just not ready to be exposed to the public, and this message has to be delivered using all the soft skills the UX researcher can muster. For example, a study we worked on for an e-commerce platform had the goal of determining whether the platform was ready to go live within the next month. The bottom line of the usability test, and our recommendation to that organization, was not to go into production with the version of the platform as it was. The launch would have taken place shortly before the Christmas period, and the planned marketing campaign would have driven a lot of people to their site. We pointed out that those customers would potentially be disappointed because the site did not offer enough products, and was quite kludgy to use. Enticing those customers to visit the site a second time (after they had implemented all the recommendations) would be more difficult if they had already formed a negative opinion about it.

We recommend sending the report out ahead of the debrief session, giving all the stakeholders ample time to review it and prepare questions.

The following are some common reactions when presenting the report for a remote usability study:

- **"This is not statistically relevant"**: We don't argue with this statement, as it is often true, and we routinely point it out at the kick-off session for the UX study. A qualitative usability study is aimed at gathering qualitative feedback and does not require large numbers to be useful or relevant.
- **"We had to do it that way because..."**: Some stakeholders will explain why a certain feature was implemented in a certain way. That does not change the fact that it is an issue for the user, and while the UX researcher should not attempt to disqualify the reasoning, he should also emphasize that the results reflect the user's perspective.
- **"Are these even the right users?"**: It is always possible that the actual participants were not the right users because they did not represent the target user groups of the product under testing. That is why we strongly recommend clarifying these profile requirements during the kick-off session, thereby avoiding this discussion after the study has been completed. The usability findings of the study nevertheless remain valid. Their severity might differ depending on the user group using the product, but it is unusual that a finding would be completely nullified.

- **"Isn't everyone in a remote study by default too digitally savvy?"**: It is near impossible to live in today's world and never have to interact with a digital interface, and as such, isn't everyone today a little bit digitally savvy? Those that actually succeed in banning all digital interfaces from their life can therefore not be the right target user group for a study aimed at evaluating the usability of a digital interface. We're being a bit facetious here. Yes, it is correct that the participants of a remote study will require some degree of digital experience in order to be able to complete a survey or record a video online, but a lot of the platforms will make this pretty transparent for the user, so no, we don't think only particularly savvy participants can participate.

- **"That usability issue is not an issue for us"**: Ok, admittedly, we've never heard this one before, but we wanted to add it for the sake of completeness. Our suggested response would be to refer back to the user feedback behind that finding and stress the user's perspective.

- **"We wouldn't want to solve that issue as per the recommendation"**: The remediation recommendations in the report are just that: recommendations. If there are compelling reasons to resolve the issue in another manner while achieving the same result, then that is fine. The main goal of any UX study is to improve the user experience. Oftentimes, UX researchers external to the organization may not be familiar with what is possible and what isn't, and this a good thing because it provides an uninfluenced view of the product under testing.

- **Conflict between stakeholders**: Conflict between stakeholders is unpleasant, but it happens. For example, the UX designer might have been arguing with the line-of-business representative over a certain feature for months and now the UX study results confirm or refute their beliefs. We recommend not to jump in right away: Let them talk and do not take sides, crossing your fingers that they will cool off quickly. If they don't, then try to wrap up that point, emphasizing again the user's perspective, and then move the conversation on to the next topic.

- **"How will this improve our bottomline?"**: Improving the usability is one factor of many that can contribute to increased conversions, decreased drop-off rates, more social media sharing, and so on. It is always beneficial to improve the usability; there is no downside to it, but it is not a guarantor that the business goals will be significantly impacted.

- **"The results seem too positive"**: Yes, there are some known reasons for participants to rate more positively. This might be because they are paid to participate in the study and want to show their appreciation; it may be because they are culturally less inclined to openly criticize, or because they think it is nicer to be nice. There is no finite way to counterbalance this. It simply has to be kept in mind when assessing the results in order to frame them correctly.

The debrief session should always end with the UX researcher asking the study sponsor whether the study was of benefit to them, and what they intend to do with the results. We also find it important to understand whether the findings were known issues or completely new to the stakeholders. Sometimes issues are known, but are not considered important until a study highlights that they make a difference to the users. This discussion is a natural segue to the organization's next steps.

Next steps

A UX study is the beginning of the first (or next) round of improvements to the product being tested. After wrapping up a study, the UX researcher should provide suggestions for potential next steps. The actual next steps will vary depending on the result of the study.

Some possible next steps may be the following:

- Update the product according to the improvement recommendations and retest to confirm that the users appreciate the improvements, and also to provide new benchmark scores to compare against the baseline of the previous test, ensuring that the product is progressing.
- Run a focused follow-up study on a particular area of the product under testing where the results may have uncovered issues and which was previously not given much attention.
- Some organizations might want to understand how their results compare with their competitors. In this case, a follow-up study could be a competitive analysis study to highlight where the organization may be better or worse than the competition.
- Maintain an archive of the usability findings that all affected stakeholders can access so that subsequent product iterations do not make the same or similar usability mistakes.

Repeat, no, stress the importance of continued usability testing and compliment the team on their user-centered approach. Lastly, be sure to keep in touch with the study sponsor and their team. Sometimes it just requires a little nudge to get the next UX study kicked off.

Summary

That's it, folks. We hope that we have enlightened you as to the benefits of remote usability testing and how to run a successful remote study. We know that remote usability testing is not the be-all and end-all of UX research, but we believe it has earned its place among the various tools, and in the right situations, it has provided our customers with valuable insights that have helped shape their products globally.

Sample Material and Further Reading

Sample material

Also check `www.sincera.eu` or `www.outriderux.com`, which are our sites, for the templates mentioned in this book:

- Kick-off session checklist
- Recruitment screener
- Discussion guides for moderated studies
- Scripts for unmoderated studies
- Observed/recorded data spreadsheet
- UX study report

Further reading

Here's a list of interesting links and references:

Data visualization

- Signal: Understanding What Matters in a World of Noise; *Stephen Few*

Forms

- Sample forms (for example, consent forms for adults and minors, digital recording release, and NDAs) and a wealth of other relevant information can be found at the Usability.gov (`https://www.usability.gov`) site

Studies with participants who use assistive tools

- Deque web accessibility training: IAAP certification course (`https://dequeuniversity.com/`)

Survey writing

- Questionnaire Design for Social Surveys: University of Michigan

Other Books You May Enjoy

If you enjoyed this book, you may be interested in these other books by Packt:

Fixing Bad UX Designs
Lisandra Maioli

ISBN: 978-1-78712-055-6

- Learn about ROI and metrics in UX
- Understand the importance of getting stakeholders involved
- Learn through real cases how to fix bad UX
- Identify and fix UX issues using different methodologies
- Learn how to turn insights and finding into practical UX solutions
- Learn to validate, test and measure the UX solutions implemented
- Learn about UX refactoring

Hands-On UX Design for Developers
Elvis Canziba

ISBN: 978-1-78862-669-9

- What UX is and what a UX designer does
- Explore the UX Process and science of making products user-friendly
- Create user interfaces and learn which tools to use
- Understand how your design works in the real world
- Create UI interaction, animation, wireframes, and prototypes
- Design a product with users in mind
- Develop a personal portfolio and be well-prepared to join the UX world

Leave a review - let other readers know what you think

Please share your thoughts on this book with others by leaving a review on the site that you bought it from. If you purchased the book from Amazon, please leave us an honest review on this book's Amazon page. This is vital so that other potential readers can see and use your unbiased opinion to make purchasing decisions, we can understand what our customers think about our products, and our authors can see your feedback on the title that they have worked with Packt to create. It will only take a few minutes of your time, but is valuable to other potential customers, our authors, and Packt. Thank you!

Index

B

budget
  about 30
  deliverables 30
  goal 30
  participants 30
  scope 30
  study methodology 30
  test environment 30

C

compensation
  about 61
  extra costs 64
  providing 63
  right amount 63
Customer Effort Score (CES) 32

D

data, findings
  column/bar chart 146, 148
  data, representing 154
  line chart 148
  lists 152
  pie chart 149
  table 151
  word cloud 151
data, summary
  bottom line 162
  goal 162
  issues 162
  optional details 162
data
  analyzing 143
  appendix 165
  audience 161

benchmark scores 163
conclusion 165
cover page 161
findings 163
findings, compiling 144
improvement/remediation recommendations 164
raw data, preparing 143
recommendations, identifying 157
report, content 161
reporting 160
study context 163
summary 162
verbatim participant comments 164
debrief session 167, 170
deliverables
  about 45
  discussion guide/script 45
  participant screener 45
  report 46
  study framework, for sign off 45
device requisites, parameters
  browsers 38
  devices 38
  product under testing, installation 38
  screen size 38
  software, installing 38
dry run
  about 77
  backup slots 77
  floaters 78
  sample schedule 78

F

findings
  compiling 145
  data, visualising 146
  interpreting 146

issues, identifying 155
observed or recorded data 145
self-reported data 145

H

hybrid method
about 136
advantage 136
device and product version confirmation 137
fraud, reducing 137
limitations 137
self-reported data, by user videos 137
UX researcher 138

I

in-person usability testing 7
issues, findings
bugs 157
false positives 157
negative or positive report 156
outliers 156
participant responses, validating 156
participants voice 156
study participants, task 155
terminology, using 156

L

lab usability testing 7

M

moderator techniques, remote moderated studies
game rules 83
note-taking 86
observers, managing 86
participants 84
monetary compensation
about 61
cash 61
donations 62
gift cards 61

N

Net Promoter Score (NPS) 33
non-monetary compensation

about 62
lottery drawings 62
promotional items 62
sheer gratitude 62
number of sessions, remote moderated studies
dry run 77
time of day 77

O

objective benchmark scores
about 32
task completion rate 32
time on task 32

P

panel companies, participants
expectations 56
target users, representation 56
participants, moderator techniques
disposition 85
level of engagement 84
participants, remote moderated studies
consistent feedback 83
participants
about 37, 39, 64
challenges 57
compensation 61
database, building for future recruiting 65
demographic requisites 37
device requisites 38
devices and tools 60
expectations 60
finding 53
incentives/compensation 41
informing 59
location 59
multiple target user groups 50
online, versus offline 59
other criteria 38
panel companies 55
re-screening participants 64
recruiting 49
screener methods 57
screening 56, 57
self-recruiting 54

study participants 53
target user groups, recruiting 51
target user profile 51
time commitments 59
pre-session tech
  setting up 80

Q

Quality Assurance (QA) 6

R

raw data
  preparing 143
  remote moderated studies 143
  remote moderated studies, with videos 144
recommendations
  alternatives, providing 159
  creating, constructive 158
  creating, direct 158
  identifying 157
  problem, solving 159
  readers' language, speaking 159
  severity, assigning 159
  usability problem, addressing 159
  user interface, using 160
remote moderated studies, tasks
  post-session questions 74
  questions 72
  task descriptions 71
  tasks and questions 70
  topics 71
  wrap-up 74
remote moderated studies
  changes, preparing 79
  communicating 78
  communicating, with observers 79
  communicating, with participants 79
  communication tools 79
  debriefing 82
  discussion guide, anatomy 68, 69
  discussion guide, creating 68
  executing 80, 104, 131, 132, 142
  internal team 76
  moderator techniques 83
  number of participants 76

number of sessions 76
participants 82
participants, scheduling 103, 131, 142
pre-session tech, setting up 80
preparing 75, 103, 131, 141
product, testing 76
session, aborting 81
session, executing 81
sessions 76
tasks 70
tips, writing 74
tool functionality 87
warm-up 69
with surveys 144
remote moderated usability testing 12
remote moderated usability testing, advantages
  about 12
  body language 13
  tailored follow-up questions 13
remote moderated usability testing, disadvantages 13
remote unmoderated usability testing 13
remote unmoderated usability testing, advantages
  about 13
  implementing 15
  influence, eliminating 14
  minors, testing 15
  natural behavior 14
  schedules, avoiding 15
  time-zone independent 14
  UX researcher 14
remote unmoderated usability testing, disadvantages
  about 15
  guidance 15
  other disadvantages 16
remote usability testing 8
remote usability testing, advantages
  about 8
  extended reach 9
  familiar equipment 10
  in-the-wild testing 11
  larger number of participants 11
  no lab costs 10
  no lab environment 10

no travel costs 9
no travel required 9
typical devices 9
user's natural environment 10
remote usability testing, disadvantages
about 11
other disadvantages 12
product under testing, distributing 11
report, deliverables
format 46
language 46
recommendations 46
topline report 46

S

script, instructions
about 96, 122
delivery 98
device, using 99, 123
product under testing, accessing 99, 122
read task instructions 99
size 98
tasks, versus questions 123
think-aloud method 97
video file format 98
video recording 98
write-down-what-you-think protocol 122
script, post-session questions 101, 126
script, post-task questions
about 101, 125
time-on-task measurement 126
script, questions created
about 127
answers 127
clarity 129
clear anchors, providing 129
facilitating sentiment expression 130
follow-up questions 130
goals 129
obvious questions 131
one question per question 128
questions, avoiding 128
task description 130
tone 129
unblocking participants 129

script, tasks
about 99, 123
complex tasks 100, 125
goal-oriented tasks 101, 125
long tasks 100, 125
task context 123
task flow 123
tasks, completing 99, 100, 124
script, tips writing
about 102
task description 102
tone 102
script
about 95, 96, 121, 122, 139
instructions 139
open questions, versus user videos 140
post-session questions 141
post-task questions 141
standalone responses 140
tasks 140
tips, writing 141
user videos, for tasks 140
video recording 140
self-recruiting, participants
coworkers 54
customers 55
friends and family 54
recruiting ads 55
session organization, user videos
number of participants 95
number of tasks 95
number of videos 95
session duration 94
session, remote moderated studies
participant, mismatching 81
participant, misrepresented 82
participant, mistmatching 81
recruited participant 82
Single Ease Question (SEQ) 32
stakeholder 22
study methodology
about 41
deadlines 42
external approval, using 44
external factors, imposing on UX study 44

moderated study 41
participants, equipped with physical devices 43
pilot run, participants/stakeholders need for 44
product, testing 42
scheduling 42
study, planning 43
survey-based studies 41
unmoderated study 41
update cycles 43
video-based studies 41
study organization, hybrid method
  about 138
  number of participants 138
  number of tasks 138
  session duration 138
subjective benchmark scores
  about 32
  Customer Effort Score (CES) 32
  Net Promoter Score (NPS) 33
  Single Ease Question (SEQ) 32
  System Usability Scale (SUS) 33
  task satisfaction rate 33
  USERindex 33
survey-based remote unmoderated study, advantages
  about 109
  deep dive questions 109
  development cycle 110
  long tasks 109
  number of participants 110
survey-based remote unmoderated study, closed questions
  grouping questions 119
  multi-answer multiple-choice questions 118
  ranking question 119
  semantic differential scale 118
  single-answer multiple-choice questions 115, 117
survey-based remote unmoderated study, limitations
  about 110
  fraud 111
  path analysis 111
  self-reported data 112
survey-based remote unmoderated study,

questions
  about 112
  closed questions 114
  open questions 113
survey-based remote unmoderated study, study organization
  about 120
  number of participants 121
  number of tasks 121
  session duration 120
survey-based remote unmoderated study
  about 108
  write-down-what-you-think protocol 108
System Usability Scale (SUS) 33

T

target user groups
  disabilities 52
  minors 51
  recruiting 51
  seniors 52
  subject matter experts 52
test environment
  about 34
  bugs 36
  product, accessing 35
  product, testing in development state 35
  requisites, adding 36
  special credentials, using 36
  target devices 34
think-aloud method, instructions
  examples 97
  greeting and task description 97
think-aloud protocol, user videos
  about 91
  continued thinking aloud 91
  formulating thoughts 91
Thinking aloud 69
tips, remote moderated studies
  style 75
  tone 75

U

usability study
  classic usability goals 29

competitors, comparing 27
concept validation 28
conversion, increasing 25
design options, comparing 26
drop-off, decreasing 25
feature validation 27
future behavior, predicting 29
global suitability 26
goal 23
measuring, against baseline 25
objective benchmark scores 32
product validation 28
scope 30
status quo, determining 24
subjective benchmark scores 32
testing 22
users, goal 26
UX study, input planning 28
usability testing methodologies
about 6
comparative studies 18
formative 17
in-person usability testing 7
lab usability testing 7
longitudinal studies 18
qualitative 17
quantitative 17

remote moderated usability testing 12
remote unmoderated usability testing 13
remote usability testing 7
single test object studies 18
single-session studies 18
study types 19
summative 17
types 16
user data
privacy 93
User Experience (UX) 6
user videos
about 90
audio capture 91
development cycle 92
Digital rights management (DRM) 93
facial expressions 92
less deliberate feedback 93
limitations 93
screen capture 90
session organization 94
strengths 92
think-aloud verbal cues 92
user actions, observation 92
video clip, displaying 92
USERindex 33
UX researcher 170

www.ingramcontent.com/pod-product-compliance
Lightning Source LLC
Chambersburg PA
CBHW080528060326
40690CB00022B/5063